MEMOIRS OF A MUSIC OBSESSIVE

Martin Warminger

First published in Great Britain by
Pen Press Publishers Ltd
The Old School
39 Chesham Road
Brighton BN2 1NB

ISBN10: 1-905621-55-8
ISBN13: 978-1-905621-55-2

Printed and bound in the UK

A catalogue record of this book is available
from the British Library

Cover design by Jacqueline Abromeit

Acknowledgements

In 1967, when I was barely out of short trousers, I joined the school book club. This was designed to give pupils the opportunity to experience the great works of English Literature. Instead, I purchased *The Art of Coarse Rugby* by Michael Green and *How to be Topp* by Geoffrey Willans and illustrated by Ronald Searle, books that I still read today. I feel that I must acknowledge the influence of these two writers who introduced me to the glorious world of comic writing and who showed me that humour can be used in any situation to be both edifying and subversive.

In the case of this book, thanks are due to many people but in particular to Mel MacLean, who did much of the original proof-reading and to Peter Thirlby and Julian Dorling who offered comments and suggestions. In addition, I am indebted to my wife, Lib, who fully supported me in this venture at a time when I was confined to the house and was probably more of a burden than she cares to admit.

I would also like to acknowledge the contribution of virtually everybody I have ever known who have, unwittingly or otherwise, provided most of the material for this book.

Lastly, my heartfelt thanks is owing to all the artists and bands mentioned in the text and many, many more besides who have created fifty years of music without which I would probably be blissfully un-obsessed.

*This book is dedicated to the memory of my Mother,
who never knew what she had started.*

Biography

Martin Warminger was born in Epsom, Surrey but now resides in Hertfordshire with his wife and two children.

Following a childhood spent in St Albans, he graduated from Reading University and qualified as a Chartered Surveyor in 1980. Based in London, he has worked in the property profession for 30 years, first as a commercial property valuer and latterly as an IT consultant.

A fan of popular music almost from birth, he still listens to an inordinate amount of it, as well as playing the guitar and writing songs as hobbies. Having amassed a vast collection of LPs and CDs over the past forty odd years, he is currently wrestling with an MP3 player and internet file downloads.

Whilst the ideas for this book were formulated over a long period of ruminating about the pop music world, the concept of committing them to paper was born during a year spent off work, recovering from a back complaint involving surgery, followed by many months of recuperation and music listening.

Contents

Introduction

I blame my grandparents. Well, my maternal grandparents anyway. You see, I've been doing a bit of thinking recently, in the way that you do when you reach a certain age, and I have come to the conclusion that it is really not my fault. Therefore, applying impeccable logic, it must be somebody else's fault. But the difficulty of pinning it onto one particular source has been the problem that has been exercising my brain.

But let's start at the beginning. I was born in the mid 1950s into a Britain emerging from post-war austerity and awakening to the burgeoning new advances in the fields of design and technology that had been set in motion by the impetus of the Festival of Britain. But, more significantly, I was born at the dawn of rock 'n' roll music, arriving in this world a little after the release of Bill Haley's 'Rock Around the Clock' and just before Elvis Presley's 'Heartbreak Hotel', and whilst there is no way of knowing how the rise of popular music, as we know it today, may have affected other people's lives, one thing is for sure; it affected mine. Astrologists will claim that an individual's fate is defined by the conjunction of planets at the moment of birth, but I prefer to believe that it was the influence of the singles chart that sealed mine. Looking at the chart for the week ending 3 March 1956, I see that I was born under the influence of Dean Martin's 'Memories are Made of This'. Well, nobody's perfect.

But the fact is I'm absolutely convinced that, at an early age, I caught from some person or persons unknown a particularly virulent form of bug that was clearly allied to the new music phenomenon. Moreover, I am now able to identify three key points in my life when it deepened its grip.

How else can I explain something that has plagued me all my life and caused me equal amounts of extreme joy, intense irritation, utter boredom, heady exhilaration, fervent hope and black despair in addition to all the other usual life stuff? Whatever it is, it is often debilitating, completely incurable and by virtue of its very presence, has provoked by turns acceptance, astonishment, admiration, suspicion and even pity in others but above all else, it has left me helplessly addicted to pop music. It is one of those afflictions that no doctor will recognise and I, myself have only come to identify my condition by careful comparison with other members of the human race. Only those that have the symptoms will be acquainted with the facts of their particular case for it is a little known ailment and as such will elicit no sympathetic response from the public at large.

Anyone who has been unfortunate enough to fall victim to this condition will immediately recognise the signs as they become apparent from an early age. They include, amongst many others, being unable to pass a music store without going in and browsing pointlessly, listening to piped music in hotel lobbies, buying the vinyl followed by the cassette followed by the CD version of all your favourite albums and *still* watching Top of the Pops. Believe me, whilst this may seem certifiable behaviour, it is only the half of it. There's sitting in your car outside your own house waiting for a particularly good song being played on the radio to end and well, you get the idea.

Whilst, as a consequence of the affliction, I have never actually felt physically unwell, unless you count that time at the Hammersmith Odeon (now Apollo) about two thirds of the way through T'pau's interminable set, the bug is ever present and has the ability to control certain behaviour patterns like invoking compulsive record buying and a strange desire to continually enthuse others about obscure albums when it is clear they have no interest at all in what you are saying.

All this malarkey is all very well when in your teens or even up to the age of thirty, but the condition continues well into middle age and possibly beyond, for all I know and at this stage of life it can be pretty embarrassing. And if you are unfortunate enough to earn a living in a predominantly middle class occupation, even more so.

And it is this feeling of final humiliation that has ultimately spurred me into tracking down its source with a view to banishing it forever, or at least, passing it on to someone else. Someone's to blame, and after much research into my past, I have managed to eliminate certain individuals from my enquiries. For example, I am pretty sure it is not my parents or any of my siblings, as I shall demonstrate and it is unlikely to be friends as this malady strikes at an early stage in your life at a time when I didn't really have any. So having reduced the suspects to remaining members of my close family, I am now in a position to lay it squarely at my grandparents' door.

Let me explain.

Chapter One

SUMMER HOLIDAY

When I was a small child in those long ago days of the early 1960s, my brother, my sister and I were routinely taken on visits to our grandparents, usually once or twice a year on an alternating schedule between maternal and paternal sets. This involved a long, winding drive across a pre-motorway south of England from St Albans, where we lived, to Chelmsford along a lattice of tree-lined 'A' class roads no wider than a car-and-a-half that, alternately, took us through green fields and tiny villages with unlikely sounding names like High Ongar and White Roding. Dependent upon our ultimate destination, this journey would provoke a sense of either indifference or anticipation. That and a feeling of travel sickness. With the usual preponderance of speed restricting heavy lorries on route, the journey would take about an hour and a quarter, but such a period of time in a car without a radio or any sort of entertainment seems archaic now when the school run cannot be contemplated without a fully stacked CD autochanger in the boot.

If our destination were my father's parents, the culmination of the journey would involve us pulling up outside a small inter-war semi located on the outskirts of Chelmsford town centre. My father had been born and raised in this house and to my childlike perception, it reeked of age. Passing over the threshold, I always received the impression that the gloomy entrance hall would have welcomed us in silence had it not been for the eerie tick tock of its imposing grandfather clock. Certainly, its dark and claustrophobic rooms seemed permanently stuck in a pre-war period of oversized furniture, porcelain figurines and valve radiograms.

Indeed, there was such a radio, placed high up on a vast walnut bureau and this seemed the only link with the modern outside world. It provoked the feeling that if it were switched on, you would hear the grave tones of Winston Churchill reading the news or the football results. But there was no music; only the drone of the BBC Home Service to which it was permanently tuned. There was no television set. There wouldn't ever be one in that house until my grandmother died in the late 1970s, it being dismissed as a product of a new unwanted technological age. So, on the face of it, it seems unlikely that I picked up any propensity for the coming musical storm that was to engulf 1960s Britain from this staid environment.

By contrast, a visit to my mother's parents involved a journey into, but then through, Chelmsford and back out into the countryside to the nearby rural settlement at Galleywood, where their newly built 1950s bungalow sat in a tiny row of similar new houses serviced by what was little more than a farm track. Drainage ditches filled with stinging nettles lined the road and an ancient farmhouse with adjoining orchard gazed balefully at the new intruders from across the road. To one side, cows grazed in fields and agricultural activities continued as they had done for centuries. On the other, a disused racecourse, its white railings still evident, created space for dog walking and adventure. (I have since returned to this area to find the house extended and land-locked by new housing estates, properly metalled roads and not a hint of the orchard, but then, the relentless march of time has no reverence where memories are concerned.)

This house was a little trickier to define. Whilst it had undoubtedly inherited some old furniture from a previous abode where my mother spent her childhood, there was a feeling of post-war design inherent in the modern light fittings, door handles and bathroom fittings. The rooms, whilst not large, were light and airy and, more to the point, there was a transistor (not valve) radio (with a big luminous dial) sitting on a kitchen cabinet and a television set in the sitting room. In fact, this television set could receive not only the BBC, but also the new fangled ITV station, a luxury to which we were not yet entitled at home. Outside, a neat garden ran from the house down to a copse of untidy trees and beyond that only fields as far as the eye could see.

In retrospect, this environment seems much more likely to have spawned an infection awakening the need to immerse myself in popular culture but the real decider was the fact that these grandparents had a Secret Weapon that would ensure the final outcome.

My auntie Gail.

My aunt was what might be described as a late child, born to elderly parents in the post-war boom almost twenty years after my mother. Consequently, she is little more than seven years older than me and, more importantly, at the time of which I now speak, she was a fully-fledged paid up member of the new order – a Teenager. Of course, in the pre-war period of my mother's childhood, teenagers didn't really exist, or if they did they didn't go around shouting about it. Gail did and it put a newly invented generation gap between not just my aunt and her parents but also between my aunt and my mother, despite their being sisters. Accordingly, this placed her firmly in the 'us' camp and not with the grownups like all my other aunts and uncles.

Furthermore, she acted in a satisfyingly teenage way by tuning the family radio (remember, the chic transistor model with the big luminous dial sitting on the kitchen cabinet) to the pirate Radio Caroline thus ensuring a diet of pop music at breakfast time at the very least, and playing loud pop records.

The effect of all this dazzling culture was most evident during the great event known as Summer Holiday at Grandma and Granddad's. For a few years this was an annual occurrence whereby my parents created a bit of space for themselves by shipping us off to Galleywood for a week in the school holidays. This meant an opportunity to see all those unknown ITV television programmes and those weird and wonderful adverts between them, to explore the racecourse with their excitable Boxer puppy and to ride into Chelmsford on the bus. But it also meant time spent with my aunt listening to records. And we did. At length.

Pop music in the early part of the 1960s was a curious beast. The initial wave of 1950s American rock 'n' roll, although still strong, had begun to subside and the frenzy of the British beat boom led by the Beatles had yet to arrive. The main contenders in the great rock 'n' roll invasion were either in the army or in jail and the impetus had faltered, at least temporarily. Consequently, in Britain at least, the decade started rather uncertainly with an unholy mixture of skiffle (am I the only person in the world who used to know all the words to 'My Old Man's a Dustman'?) and ballads from the likes of Max Bygraves and Jimmy Young. All was not lost, however, and my aunt had unerringly sought out the best stuff such as singles by The Shadows, Adam Faith, Cliff Richard, the Joe Meek stable of acts and her own personal favourite, Billy Fury.

For someone still at infants' school, this was all heady stuff and a world away from my own parents' meagre record collection (total: 6 LPs and a motley assortment of 7-inch singles). During my deliberations as to whom to blame for my current obsessions, I considered my parents' role carefully and came to the conclusion they had very little effect at all. Neither were particularly musical and neither sang nor played an instrument. Sadly, my mother's only contribution to my musical education was the existence of a 'Best of Pat Boone' LP and a couple of singles in the family collection, which I found virtually unlistenable. From my father I inherited a passing interest in traditional jazz, but no interest at all in the light musicals which, to my horror, he admitted in later life to having a lifelong affection. Perhaps the inclusion in our paltry family collection of the 'My Fair Lady' soundtrack LP should have been a clue, but it had no impact at the time.

On the plus side, we did own a modern radio which sat in the kitchen and was tuned to the BBC light programme. This provided us with Two-way family favourites before Sunday lunch and the chart rundown on that same afternoon. But on the whole, there was little impetus gained from the home environment. Quite how all three of us children came to learn musical instruments and become embroiled in popular music culture from such inauspicious beginnings remains a minor miracle.

Meanwhile, back at Galleywood, progress was being made. In my aunt's bedroom, there stood a solid wooden cabinet that looked and felt like a sort of proto safe, before someone had the bright idea that metal would make a more secure building material. It was almost impossible to open as the door fitted with such perfection that the air inside seemed to create a vacuum when the handle was pulled. Inside, the space was divided into sections by vertical wooden partitions and each surface was covered with green baize. Every space was stuffed full of vinyl records – 7-inch singles, 12-inch LPs and even a few 10-inch 78s. Because the cabinet was almost air tight, it allowed no aroma leakage and when the door was opened an almost overpoweringly heady smell of vinyl and warm cardboard issued forth.

This must have been the first of those three key moments in my life when the defences are lowered and the bug strikes. The other two defining moments would follow a little later but this was the most devastating. There is just something about the smell and the feel of a vinyl record and its paper or cardboard sleeve, especially from that era when the vinyl was thicker and more brittle, that makes it such a sensual and desirable object. I think I fell in love with records as objects before I fell in love with the music they contained but it wasn't long before I had succumbed to both. The combination of the sensual and musical was an irresistible combination and I was hooked.

Having selected a disc, it was carried ceremoniously to the radiogram in the sitting room to be played. Disappointingly and unlike the modern transistor radio and the television set, the record playing equipment came from the dark ages, or possibly before. How my aunt could have allowed this, I really don't know. A well-known side effect of the music bug is the desire to buy newer and better playing equipment. Anyway, there it stood, a vast dark wood monolith, brooding in the corner of the room. Nevertheless, it contained a serviceable auto-change record deck, valve amplifier, radio tuner and a single huge loudspeaker. The sound, whilst not lacking in volume, was, well interesting in a sort of all bass and very little else sort of way. Listening to any sound source from it was akin to what I imagine a drowning person would hear if someone was shouting to them from the bank – a sort of distant flow of words engulfed in a wallowing, muffling swooshing. No matter, it was wonderful.

My aunt would play all her favourites at ridiculous volume and resembling a miniature mini-skirted Mary Quant with a bee somewhere in her clothing, would try to entice me to dance the twist, or some other new craze. Even at the tender age of six, I instinctively knew that white middleclass males just didn't dance and so, attempted to keep my distance and my dignity. It didn't always work.

In later visits I would take my 'lyric book'. This was an old exercise book that I had filled with lyrics, painstakingly researched from listening to the radio for weeks on end. In it, I had compiled what I thought to be complete sets of lyrics to songs of the day like The Searchers' 'Needles and Pins' and Freddie and the Dreamers' 'You Were Made for Me'. The reason why this document accompanied me was that my aunt had acquired the use of a reel-to-reel tape recorder. This amazing device was, to me, straight from science fiction in that it played back this strange sounding voice that people would tell you was yours but sounded more like an alien from the outer reaches of the galaxy. It was a vast cream-coloured box with two huge spools and clunky mechanical levers that took the strength of Hercules to operate. Now, my aunt had a friend; a girl called Melanie who would come round from time to time and it was then that the two girls had some fun with the tape recorder. One of their favourite games was to sing pop songs into the microphone and then collapse into gales of laughter at the result, hence the need for my lyric book. Unfortunately, my transcriptions were not as accurate as I had imagined and it often left the singers fumbling for a missing syllable or two, or trying to cram too many words into a line, but this only added to the fun. Luckily, nobody thought to ask me to sing.

At this point I am relying on hearsay, as I was clearly too young to remember, but I am reliably informed that my earliest favourite single was 'Living Doll' by Cliff Richard (the 1959 original, not the abomination with the Young Ones). So enamoured of this song was I that it was bought for me. I still have it. It still displays its now rather faded green Columbia label with a red sticker to identify the 'A' side and sits snugly inside its pyjama striped Columbia sleeve. As usual for this period, the sleeve contains a series of advertisements for the company's long-playing records on the non-striped side. In this instance we are urged to purchase such gems as offerings from Big Ben Banjo Band and Norrie Paramor and his Orchestra. It is with some shame that I admit that the former offering was already in our family collection and pretty dire it was, too.

To most people, this piece of scratched and rather shabby vinyl is just another bit of throwaway junk, but in fact it is a slice of history, belonging to me personally and to everyone in general. It's part of my history because it links me with my own past. I know every note played by every instrument on that disk and when I play it now, as I do from time to time, I am transported back to my childhood and the times that it was played either with my aunt or on my own at home, embarrassing dancing and all. But, more importantly, it is part of everyone's history. The invention of sound recording in the late nineteenth century has allowed man to stop time for a short period and capture it. When you listen to 'Living Doll' what you are hearing is Cliff's actual performance of that song, as it happened, nearly fifty years ago. Not a third party description, as you may find in a book describing the event, or a review in a magazine, but the event itself. The listener is hearing exactly the performance that the recording engineer heard at the time standing perhaps a few yards away from the performer. This is true of all songs recorded in the 1950s and 1960s but, sadly, it probably does not apply to the majority of songs we hear today. Modern digital technology has allowed record producers to edit together definitive performances from several attempts, but in principle we are still hearing a slice of time captured for future generations.

The more you think about this concept, the scarier it becomes. The generations of man to come in the centuries stretching before us will be able to hear this performance long after Cliff and everyone else involved with the recording is dead. Even now, we are able to hear actual speech recordings of people such as George Bernard Shaw and Florence Nightingale made in the latter part of the nineteenth century, but imagine what it would be like to hear recordings of say, the signing of Magna Carta or the coronation of Henry the Eighth. In reality this is exactly the sort of experience that will be available to man far into the future. He will be able to hear recordings made centuries before he was born and almost relive history rather than just read about it.

I've always understood, in a naïve sort of way, that the science fiction of time travel really only involves catching up with and getting in front of light that has disappeared off into space and 'seeing' it again. All events emit light – some of which enters our eyes when we see that event happening and the remainder zooms off into space. Hence in order to see past events, we must travel faster than light in order to catch up with a particular piece of light and let it re-enter our eyes. What we really need is a device that captures that light and holds it here on earth. But we have one. It is called the camera. Hence, the still camera and more recently the moving image camera have allowed us to time travel by capturing not just sound but pictures too, so that in the example cited above, we would be able to see, as well as hear, King John signing away his power, but this discussion is outside the remit of this book.

The other aspect of historical context relates to the content of this record. The 'A' side, 'Living Doll' is basically a show tune, written by Lionel Bart for the film 'Serious Charge' and comprises a mid-paced ballad arranged by the Drifters (Cliff's backing band at the time, before changing their name to the Shadows) for the now obligatory line-up of guitar, bass and drums with a dash of piano. However, its sound, based around string bass and offbeat snare drum, although not unusual for the time, harks back to an earlier age of smoky jazz clubs. I'm sure the guitarist used one of those early semi-solid electric guitars, a sound that I now love, to fashion the languid solo, just like countless jazz guitarists before him.

But flip the disk over and the 'B' side gives away its place in the history of popular music. Here we have an uptempo ditty called 'Apron Strings'. The suave relaxed croon of 'Living Doll' has vanished and in its place we have a much earthier, more urgent performance containing virtually all the vocal inflections of one Elvis A Presley. You can almost see the lip curl, so astute is the impersonation. The rhythm is relentless and guitars snarl around a pounding bass line. At once, the implication is clear: in the Britain of 1959 the post-war big band and crooner sound may be OK for some, but rock 'n' roll is here to stay and if you don't keep a foot in that camp it could be all over for you, Cliff included. As we now know, it wasn't and Cliff became a big star by developing his own style, which tended to transcend most fads but this early record shows the powerful influence that American culture was beginning to have on these shores in the late 1950s. In essence, my humble record captures the moment between the continuation of the old guard and the heralding of the new in two three-minute songs. Who would have thought that such a throwaway consumer object could carry so much meaning?

Back in June 2004 there was an incident that throws a new perspective on the question of musical history. I first became aware of Tony Blackburn whilst listening to that brand new transistor radio when he was broadcasting from one of the pirate radio stations during the sixties. Having not listened to his recent programmes, I was amazed to learn that he was almost put in the absurd position of losing his job on Capital Gold, a noted 'oldies' radio station, for playing Cliff Richard records where the station policy was to ignore them. Ironically, Blackburn was not playing recent rather turgid Cliff singles, against which, presumably, the ban was designed to protect listeners' delicate sensibilities, but those from the sixties. Let us be clear here, I have long since ceased to be a Cliff Richard fan. My interest in his work faded after about 1970, but there is no doubt that in the early sixties, he was a force to be reckoned with in the face of the American onslaught. Singles such as 'The Young Ones', 'Summer Holiday' and 'Bachelor Boy' are all bright, uplifting pop songs in the tradition that still exists today among the likes of Britney Spears and Justin Timberlake. Why is it that authorities in charge of the music industry in all its forms always seem to get it so wrong, so often? There is a sad inevitability about policy decisions that seek to blanket ban artists on the basis that they are no longer appealing, only to succeed in practice, in disallowing listeners the chance to hear material drawn from the artists' relevant work. After all, what's wrong with playing old records on an oldies station? Or have I missed something here?

Contemplating these nostalgic memories about Cliff and the others that formulated my early interests has led me to the following conclusions. It is now perfectly clear that my current obsessions were nothing to do with my immediate family or me but that my formative years spent in the company of my aunt was the catalyst that led to a life in thrall to the music business and all its quirks. I loved it then in all innocence but what I hadn't bargained for was that the journey had only just begun.

Chapter Two

THE WINNER TAKES IT ALL

Lists. We music fanatics just love lists. We can debate them for hours and obsess about minutiae until the cows come home, or the pub shuts, whichever is the sooner. Making lists is a national occupation, at least for the male of the species and is the one thing guaranteed to cause fervent debate and controversy as there is never a right answer, only opinion. But even in the context of opinion, there are problems of definition, as I shall, I hope, demonstrate.

My association with lists started when I was a child, poring over the singles chart, but it reached maturity when I was a radio listener during my university years. In 1976, Capital Radio in London polled its listeners to produce the 'Top 100 Songs of all Time'. At the time, I found this exercise absolutely fascinating for the simple reason that I had not heard it done before outside of the classic pub argument and was genuinely interested in the result. If I remember correctly, the winner was 'I'm not in Love' by 10cc. OK, not my choice, but it fired the imagination and the study and production of lists has become *de rigueur* for any self-proclaimed music buff. Nick Hornby wrote a whole novel based on it.

In recent times we have been positively deluged with the things. Every month the music magazines are awash with lists. Radio and television shows bore us with three-hour spectaculars of every type of countdown imaginable. In the recordings category, we are treated to the eminently reasonable 'top 100 albums' and 'top 100 singles' every now and again. Then there's the slightly more desperate, 'top 100 punk singles', 'top 100 singles since 1980', 'top 100 British acid house albums' and so on and so on, and finally we descend to the truly bizarre, such as 'top 100 singles that contain a flute solo'. Actually, I made that last one up but hey, there's a thought. Let me see:

1. California Dreamin' – Mamas and Papas
2. You've Got to Hide Your Love Away – Beatles
3. Living in the Past – Jethro Tull
4. Nights in White Satin – Moody Blues
5. Err…

You see? This is the rub: they're just so damn addictive.

But what is it about lists that sends us obsessives into paroxysms of anticipation at the outset and then to inevitable frustration and ultimate depression? Why don't the results of these surveys seem to have any coherence? Why do we get the slightly uneasy feeling that works by the Beatles and say, Boney M, should not be standing shoulder to shoulder in the same list, despite sales evidence to the contrary?

Addictiveness aside, there are many other problems inherent in the compilation of such lists. But in particular, there is one major problem that bedevils all lists and it is this: what, *exactly*, does the survey purport to provide? What, if asked to vote for 'the top 5 LPs of all time', do you understand by it? What does anyone think they are providing when they fill in these sorts of surveys? When I was at school and about to sit another raft of examinations, I was told to read the question, then read the question again and then answer it, the implication being that unless I knew what the question was asking, I didn't stand a chance of answering it correctly and thus would forfeit the educational institution of my choice, or worse. Applying this infallible logic to the subject of music lists would probably result in something like this:

Scene: A vast, empty, draughty hall containing a single desk and chair. I'm sitting at it with pen and paper at the ready. There is a printed A4 sheet faced down on the desk. Somewhere, a clock is ticking remorselessly.

Distant Voice: Turn over your question paper, now. You have one hour to complete it.

Me: Hmm. Oh God! Just relax and read the question. It says; 'Create a list of the top 5 long playing records of all time (100 marks)'. No other questions! It's a doddle! I'll just dash this off in a couple of minutes and then look smug for the remaining time. Here goes.

1. Sgt Pepper's Lonely Hearts' Club Band – Beatles
2. Pet Sounds – Beach Boys
3. OK Computer – Radiohead
4. Blood On The Tracks – Bob Dylan
5. Automatic For The People – REM

That looks OK. I suppose I could have had 'Revolver' for 'Sgt Pepper', but it's a moot point. Not sure whether I should have had REM in there but what else is there? Velvet Underground? U2? Van Morrison? Hendrix? No, this will do.

My Conscience: Very good. I assume we own all these records, do we?

Me: Well, no, actually.

My Conscience: So how do we know that they're any good?

Me: Because they're classics aren't they? Everyone says they're great so they must be. You don't have to *own* a record just to know it's good, do you? This is a list of what I consider to be the worthiest records of all time on the basis of general critical acclaim, as required by the question.

My Conscience: I see. So even though we don't own half of them, we've listened to them all, have we?

Me: Well, no. Not exactly. In fact, I've never listened to any Dylan albums at all – can't stand the bloke. But I'm sure they must be OK. He's an icon.

My Conscience: I'm sorry, but I am not allowing any entries that we have neither heard nor own, on the basis that we are in no position to judge anything not personally known to us. Surely the question implies this?

Me: Oh, all right. Let's have a think. I've still got loads of time. Yes, got it. In that case it will have to be:

1. Abbey Road – Beatles
2. A Night At The Opera – Queen
3. OK Computer – Radiohead
4. The Dark Side Of The Moon – Pink Floyd
5. The Queen is Dead – Smiths

Phew! No problem. I own all of these and they are critically acclaimed and the list still looks like I know what I'm talking about. Brilliant!

My Conscience: Just out of interest, do we play these records a lot?

Me: Not much, admittedly. In fact, I think the Beatles one is still in the loft somewhere – I must get it down. Oh yes, and I lent the Smiths one to someone about ten years ago and never got it back.

My Conscience: So this list doesn't really represent our favourite, can't-bear-to-take-it-off-the-turntable category records, does it?

Me: Well if you're going to be picky, I suppose not. But they are still critically acclaimed albums, experts would agree, *and* I own them and I *have* listened to them. What more do you want?

My Conscience: Sorry, but I'm not convinced. My reading of the question is that we need to compile a list of five of our favourite and by this I mean *most played* records. Not just the ones that we feel *ought* to be there.

Me: Yes, fair comment, but if that sort of information got out, I'd be a laughing stock. Look, we've only got ten minutes left now! Quickly.

1. Court and Spark – Joni Mitchell
2. Rumours – Fleetwood Mac
    Distant Voice: Five minutes left!
    Me: Bloody Hell! Err…
3. Debut – Björk
4. Like a Prayer – Madonna
5. Born To Run – Bruce Springsteen

There! I play all these quite a lot and I escape with my credibility intact.

My Conscience: Y-e-s, but they're not *really* the ones that we play all the time, are they?

Me: (silence)

My Conscience: *Are they??*

Me: No.

My Conscience: Well, I still think that the question requires...

Me: All right! ALL RIGHT!!

1. Mental Notes – Split Enz
2. Scoundrel Days – A-ha
3. A Secret Wish – Propaganda
4. Split – Lush

Err...

Distant Voice: Pens down!

Me: AAAAARRRRRRRGGGGHHHHHHH!!!!!

So you see the problem? What exactly are these 'Top' lists asking us to provide. Is it:

a) Any recordings we think ought to be there because the consensus of critical acclaim agrees that they are the dog's whatsits even though we personally wouldn't buy them at a car boot?

b) Similar to (a) above but limited only to those we own and therefore know something about?

c) A selection of recordings that we own and believe have some value even though we don't personally like them and that must be right because neither did that bloke from X magazine (insert music publication of choice) when he reviewed it?

d) Those that we play constantly even though they would see our personal credibility go through the floor if anyone ever found out?

e) Black Lace's entire back catalogue?

And the answer is, in the manner of most magazine quizzes: all of them. The question never specifies. The truth is, no one knows what the hell they are doing, everyone has their own agenda and that is why these lists are so confused and ultimately such a complete and utter waste of space. Any competent scientist will tell you that in order to conduct a meaningful experiment, that which is to be tested or discovered must be carefully defined and all other conditions controlled. Anything less and the results are meaningless. And this is what bugs me to the nth degree about all this palaver, because I really, really want to know what people think about our musical heritage. I am itching to know which songs, albums, etc are the nation's favourites, but there has to be some sort of proper definition applied at the kick-off if the result is to mean anything. So, having got that off my chest, what do I propose doing about it? Having conducted some extensive research and canvassed the opinions of others I would suggest the following. I would split the 'Top 100 songs/albums of all time' type scenario into two separate lists and ask prospective pollsters two questions:

My first question would be:

Q) What are the recordings that you judge to have the highest artistic merit?

In this case, you need not own any of them, nor should you have necessarily heard all of them. Obviously, this would help, but it is not a prerequisite. You need not even like any of them, but you must feel that they have some absolute merit. For example, the Beatles' Sgt. Pepper is not one of my favourite albums, but I can appreciate that, for its time, it is highly imaginative and has tremendous historical importance. This question is asking us to be objective assessors so as to, hopefully, produce a list of the most artistically important recordings ever. This would be called 'The Merit List'. I would add the condition that no recording made in the five years prior to the poll be included for the reason that any sort of objective judgement requires a distance perspective. For this reason I would not expect the list to change markedly from one year to the next as quality doesn't really change, but to evolve slowly as memories of older recordings fade and new contenders appear.

My second question would be:

Q) What are the recordings that you judge to be your own personal favourites?

In this case, you must own them and they must be the ones that you play the most. They must not, and I repeat not, be the ones that you feel *ought* to be your favourites. This is the crunch. This is the moment when you have to stop pretending that you have 'Pet Sounds' permanently playing on your iPod and face the reality that your favourites and indeed most people's favourites have more modest artistic claims. This question is designed to produce a subjective list of the nation's favourite recordings at a given point in time, irrespective of artistic or commercial merit. This would be called 'The Favourites List'. In this instance there is no time bar. All recordings qualify, from the year dot to the day before the poll, as it is all to do with current preferences. For this reason, the list would be much more volatile and I would expect it to be far more changeable than the Merit List.

As you will have gathered by now, I have come to the conclusion that the basic flaw with these types of 'Top' lists is that they are a confused mess comprising a conglomeration of those items that some of us feel ought to be represented, thus reaffirming our own intellectual prowess and street credibility, and those that others of us genuinely like but are a little sheepish about saying so. As such, the resultant list falls between two stools labelled 'Objective' and 'Subjective' with a resounding thud and ends up being a representation of neither. The solution, I submit, is as described above. That is, to separate the lists so that on the one hand, we can be as pompous as we choose in a man-in-the-pub way and end up with the objective Merit List, an artistic list bursting with recordings chock-full of integrity and significance that few people actually listen to. Or, on the other hand, we can indulge ourselves and be as silly as we like in a furtive-mad-dance-to-'Le Freak' way and end up with the subjective Favourites List, crammed full of holiday dance tunes and that thing that Wayne and Roxanne played at their wedding and was such a scream. Anyway, here's hoping.

Whilst this proposal goes a long way towards solving the problem of mixed objectivity and subjectivity, it does not help in the case where a list is being used for a specific purpose. For example, an albums Merit list compiled for the specific purpose of identifying the great and the good will miss all artists whose forte is singles, rather than albums and here I am thinking of, in particular, Madness. By common consent, there are no real killer Madness albums, yet they are, also by common consent, one of the greatest singles bands ever, having produced a string of 15 top ten tunes over a 5-year period. Conversely, those artists that have several classic albums to their name will also be misrepresented, as it is inevitable that their vote will be split between each candidate. The category of artist that tends to benefit in this situation is the one that released only one classic album – like Love's 'Forever Changes', or the Human League's 'Dare'. Statistics not only prove most contentions, they are equally adept at leaving out others.

There are several other reasons why 'Top' lists fail. The first is that it becomes quite apparent that there is inevitably a form of thought inertia acting once the list cycle has been put in motion. Presumably, there is some sort of physical law that governs this effect but I'm damned if I can remember what it is, being asleep for most of my Physics education. In any event, I think I shall invent one. So, Warminger's First Law of Music Lists states that 'once a list has been published, all subsequent lists will resemble the first almost exactly. This state will continue either to infinity or until the demographic of the compilers has changed'. In practice, what happens is that we all see the first list and then when asked the same question again, immediately think back to the original for inspiration rather than think anew. It's human nature to be lazy. The effects of Warminger's First Law are twofold. First, the pool of candidates for any subsequent list is immediately reduced to approximately the content of the first list thus perpetuating it and second, if any recording was left out of the first list by some disastrous oversight, it is extremely unlikely that it will ever feature again, as it will have already entered a timeless blind spot. Even if those questioned subsequently suddenly remember it in a flash of inspiration, the reasoning will go something like: 'It wasn't in the last list, so it can't be that good, can it?' Conversely, stuff that should never have been there in the first place will hang around like a bad smell contaminating all subsequent attempts to get it right.

Alternatively, the effects of Warminger's Second Law of Music Lists are felt. This law states that 'in certain bizarre circumstances most of the compilers will be unable to remember anything that happened more than three years prior to the date of the list'. The result is that the list then becomes inundated with chart material from the previous year or so, to the detriment of great songs or albums from the long and varied history of rock. This phenomenon has become more pronounced as new generations have progressively less and less interest in music or its history and thus vote only for what they remember from the immediate past. The worst situation arises when both the First and Second laws apply and we end up with a list of statutory favourites, interspersed with also rans from the last week's chart.

The second failure point is altogether more sinister and it tends to occur not so much in your common or garden list, but in these big nationwide polls that the media like to indulge in when the final placings are to be announced on television or at awards ceremonies. In these cases, the list is overtly advertised as 'chosen by the people' but when the small print is diligently perused, it turns out that a sample of say, fifty recordings have been picked behind the scenes by 'Experts' and all the public has to do is *pick from the list,* thus creating the final order of preference. Of course, under no circumstances can this be deemed to be a people's poll but rather an underhand way of guiding the result to suit a few and passing it off as chosen by the many.

At the time of writing, we have just witnessed this skulduggery in action at the Brit Awards. Being the twenty-fifth anniversary of this annual awards ceremony, some bright spark had the idea of choosing the 'Best song from the last twenty-five years' as chosen by the public, naturally. What the public was actually allowed to do was pick their favourite from a list of twenty-five candidates already whittled down from the hundreds of contenders by, yes you've guessed it, experts. Who are these experts? What criteria did they use to pick the contenders? Did they compensate for the effect of Warminger's First Law? What we really want to see in these circumstances is a totally open vote (Warminger's Laws notwithstanding), but then who would relish the job of standing up in front of the entire music industry and a huge television audience to announce that the winner is 'Shaddap You Face' by Joe Dolce? Perhaps there is some method in the almost absurdly controlling procedure, after all.

And while we're about it, how come I never get to be consulted when the votes are cast? I've lost count of the number of times that I have become aware of a new list, either in a magazine on television or radio, only to be told in no uncertain terms that it was voted for by 'you, the public'. Well, nobody asked me. Where was I when all this canvassing was going on? Did I sleep through it? Here I am, gagging to be involved and yet never seem to have the chance. The answer, I realise, is that at any given time, I read the wrong newspapers, belong to the wrong clubs and listen to the wrong radio programmes. Voting in national polls is extraordinarily secular. I fully expect the next nationwide 'Top albums of all time' poll to be drawn from patrons of the public bar of the Dog & Ferret, Barnsley (including Landlord's dog). It'll probably be more interesting than most.

Whilst list mania appears to be a modern phenomenon, there is evidence of its presence as far back as the 1970s when DJ Nicky Horne would invite listeners to phone in to his evening show on Capital Radio and submit song titles based on a set daily subject. My only memory of this ad hoc list creation scheme was under the subject, 'Music for

Dentists' when one wag phoned in with Genesis' 'Get 'em out by Friday'.

But when all is said and done and despite all their faults, the most exasperating thing is that I just *know* that I shall still be on tenterhooks waiting for the results of the next survey or award or whatever. That is the endless fascination with lists and I don't think there's a cure.

Chapter Three

GLAD ALL OVER

I suppose that my formative years, those years in the very early 1960s that I can barely remember now, must have primed me for the big event. Like some ancient prophet, I somehow knew that one day something big would come and come it did. It was late in 1963 when the Beatles hit suburban St Albans in a big way.

'She Loves You' echoed around the school playground for weeks. There was a buzz about the new sound. This wasn't just another pop song – it was electric, breathless and new. The Beatles were to change everything and even at this stage, there were enough indications to predict this outcome. We Young Ones seemed to know it instinctively but even our teachers knew it, judging by the snippets of overheard conversation between classes. Something was happening and I knew that I wanted to be part of it.

This was undoubtedly the second key point in my life when the music bug bit deeper and I was well on my way to addiction. As it transpired, 'being part of it' actually translated into 'buying a lot of records and being ridiculed for the rest of your life' and not much more, but who wants to be a multi-million pound rock star anyway? But being part of it *then* was a lot of fun. It meant drawing guitar strings and frets on your ruler and singing the Hollies' 'Stay' at the top of your voice at playtime, holding snap polls as to your favourite Beatle and avidly collecting pop star cards from the ice cream van.

The housing estate that I grew up on was constructed in the late 1950s on farmland just to the north of the urban limit of St Albans, an historic market town in Hertfordshire. Our family were the first occupiers of a semi-detached house situated on the outer ring of the estate with views over farmland stretching away from the bottom of our garden. The primary school I attended had also been newly constructed a few years before I rolled up on a cold February morning in 1961 and comprised the usual flat-roofed, glass and steel structure that most schools of that vintage resemble. My earliest musical memory is that of walking into morning assembly every day to the strains of Schubert's 'Trout Quintet', playing on a brand new record player that sat in a tubular frame on castors. The school was obviously so new that it only possessed one record, or so it seemed as I don't have any memory of anything else ever being played during those mornings. In fact, the ever-present Trout Quintet turned up in our music lessons as well where our music teacher explained the story of the fisherman angling for the trout and how the music becomes more dramatic as he stirs up the water to confuse the fish. At this point our teacher showed us the music manuscript to enforce the contention that, as a result of all this escalation, the page was 'black with music'. I always remember that phrase, as it sounded dramatic and mysterious even though I didn't really understand what it meant. Such are the unconnected building blocks that imperceptibly construct an interest in a subject. Years later, during a run of the television programme 'The Goodies', there was an episode where the Goodies open their own radio station, but only possess one record, 'A Walk in the Black Forest' which they play repeatedly. I imagine that they must have based this episode on my primary school.

As it turned out, the following year, 1964, was to be a bumper year for great number one singles. The list included; 'Glad All Over' – The Dave Clark Five, 'Needles and Pins' – The Searchers, 'Oh Pretty Woman' – Roy Orbison, 'Anyone Who Had a Heart' – Cilla Black, 'House of the Rising Sun' – The Animals, 'You Really Got Me' – The Kinks, 'Baby Love' – Supremes, 'It's All Over Now' – The Rolling Stones, plus *four* more Beatles singles. As an introduction to what was to become a lifelong obsession, you'd be hard pushed to beat it.

That summer, the Warminger family decamped to Gorleston-on-Sea, near Great Yarmouth for our annual holiday. The Beatles had just released their album 'A Hard Day's Night' to accompany the film of the same name and it blasted out on continuous loop from the pier and from every amusement arcade. So intoxicating was it that I didn't even notice the usual bitter wind whipping off the North Sea. To me, life at that moment was lived to a Beatles' soundtrack.

1964 was also the year when a new, weekly pop music television programme started to be broadcast on the BBC: Top of the Pops. For a newly signed-up member of the pop culture revolution, this was essential viewing. However, to one who was already addicted to music lists at the tender age of eight, there was one serious flaw in TOTP and for a time it caused some consternation. During the programme, the resident DJ of the week, by turns Jimmy Savile, David Jacobs, Pete Murray and Alan Freeman would introduce each record and then play it (no worries about miming in those days). To do this link the participant stood in front of a large chart showing the week's Top Twenty records. The problem was that I couldn't memorise the entire twenty records and therefore was at a loss to remember who was, for example, number 15 or number 8 in the record sales chart from one week to the next. What if somebody asked me? These sorts of things mattered.

After much thought, the answer was clear: I had to construct a similar chart that could be kept in my room for reference and which I could change from week to week. This was accomplished using cardboard from old cereal packets. I was a bit of a whiz at using cereal packet cardboard as a building material. So much so, in fact, that our larder always contained several waxed bags of uneaten cereal, the cardboard packet long ago transformed into a model of Fireball XL5 or my own version of Monopoly.

Anyway, the completed chart was made in two sections, a solid back sheet and a front sheet with twenty numbered slots cut into it. These were glued together in such a way that cardboard tabs with the song name and artist written on them could be slid between them and held in place under each slot. Using my patent chart I could pore over chart positions all week, and then update the song positions at the next programme. In reality, the update procedure was often fraught with difficulty, as there were only six or seven links in each show when the BBC chart was on view. Also, and more problematical, the DJ of the week would stand in front of the chart, rendering its lower half from about number 13 downwards invisible unless there was a brief sideways movement of the body, at which juncture, I had to memorise as many of the placings as I could in that split second in a manner not unlike the Generation Game conveyor belt. Clearly, the height of the DJ for any particular week was also a determining factor. Pete Murray was too tall and obscured more of the chart than, say, Jimmy Savile. Jimmy also spoke for longer which was a positive boon; hence his weeks were to be easier on the memory than the others. Frankly, the whole exercise became so frantic that I was hugely relieved when the Top Twenty was eventually published in one of the daily newspapers.

In one corner of the estate where we lived, there was a row of newly built shops, one of which sold records, and in its window a top twenty chart appeared suddenly overnight. Worryingly, it differed from the one shown on TOTP, but nevertheless it added a stamp of authority that us list fanatics could point to when pop charts were brought into disrepute by our elders, that is, most of the time. The fact that you could buy singles so close to home was a tantalising thought, but for me at that time on a tiny sweet-buying income, it was always a forlorn hope. Still, I did have my copy of 'Living Doll' to play, along with my mother's copy of Frank Ifield's 'I Remember You'. Cliff and a yodeller would have to do for the moment.

Have you noticed how, almost without fail, whenever anybody even remotely famous is asked to name the first single they ever bought it turns out to be something from the all time list of greatest singles ever? If it's not 'Strawberry Fields Forever', it's 'Thriller' or 'Bohemian Rhapsody'. Why is it that for the rest of us mere mortals, it is always something from the most cringeworthy list of all time and we'd rather not say, thank you. The infuriating thing is: I could have been one of them. I could have been up there with those that have no fear of the dreaded question and could answer nonchalantly, 'Yes, actually it was 'A Whiter Shade of Pale' by Procol Harum. I remember it well.'

And it could have been, if it had not have been one of the best selling singles at the time.

In my final year at Primary school, a disco was arranged as a farewell party for all those leaving at the end of the summer term. The school hall was decked out in streamers and balloons, soft refreshments were laid on and I duly turned up to not dance, as usual. During the proceedings a new record was played, which turned out to be the aforesaid 'A Whiter Shade of Pale'. The one with the strangely evocative lyrics that no one really understands and the pseudo Bach melody. So entranced with this new sound was I that I badgered my parents for weeks afterwards to buy it for me. By this time it was the number one single in the country and would stay there for many weeks. In the end, after some negotiation, a deal was struck whereby I would use my meagre pocket money and my father would make up the balance. Thus, clutching my seven shillings and sixpence (37.5p for younger readers), I legged it to the local record store on the following Saturday morning and strode confidently up to the counter.

'A Whiter Shade of Pale, please.'

'Sorry, mate, we've sold out.'

Oh God. I could feel my stomach churning. What to do? I couldn't go home empty-handed and being in my usual highly pitched state of record purchasing frenzy, I decided that I couldn't let this setback deter me. I searched my mind frantically for something else I liked whilst smiling inanely at the shop assistant. Seconds seemed like weeks as I desperately tried to think. Finally:

'Er, in that case, have you got 'Alternate Title' by the Monkees?

'Sure. That'll be seven and six.

So there you have it. The first single that I ever (half) bought by myself was by the Monkees. My parents never forgave me for wasting their money and further subsidies were severely curtailed. Whether this was because they secretly liked 'A Whiter Shade of Pale' or whether they thought the Monkees a waste of money (probably both), I shall never know. The real agony was that it wasn't even one of their better singles. It might at least have been one of their finer moments like 'I'm a Believer' or 'Last Train to Clarksville' or something. And to think, I was *this* close.

Mind you, I liked going into record shops and did so on any excuse. The one in St Albans was called 'The Record Room' and was a tiny, narrow affair with two frontages so that you could go in one door and out the other at the back. It had a small counter and a couple of listening booths that I could never quite pluck up the courage to use. But it had an otherworldly atmosphere that shops don't seem to have now. The walls were liberally plastered with weird psychedelic posters from the sixties overlaid with scruffy bits of paper with sale or wanted advertisements scrawled on them, such as 'Wanted, drummer, must be into Hendrix, Cream and T Rex'. That's assuming you could see them, the lighting being so low that infrared glasses were needed. Wooden racks held masses of bent record sleeves in plastic covers that browsers could pore over. I could spend all afternoon in this shop and sometimes did. I think I knew the stock better than the owner and I always knew when something new had arrived. Most of the large music stores today seem clinically clean, fresh and over bright, but there are still a few Aladdin's caves to be found in city back streets where, if you peer through the gloom you can read wanted ads saying 'Wanted, drummer, must be into Hendrix, Cream and McFly'.

Buying singles was fun and I saved my pocket money for weeks just to experience the thrill of their purchase. My school friend, Terry, and I would cycle into town once a month, prop our bikes up in the alley next to the Record Room and proudly purchase a single each. In this way I collected stuff like Elton John's 'Your Song', Diana Ross's 'Ain't No Mountain High Enough' and others. If I was feeling particularly impoverished, I would check out the Market stalls on a Saturday where you could pick up ex-juke box singles cheaply. The downside of this pastime was that the records were old, scratched and had their 'spider' centres removed, requiring the use of an adapter if they were to be played on a standard spindle record player.

But singles collection was more than fun, it was educational. There were many areas of the new fangled rock 'n' roll that were still a closed book to me and one of them was guitar solos. Whilst I was quite happy to hum along with the sort of innocuous solo that would fill eight bars or so in the middle of a decent song, I just couldn't get my head around anything that involved effects like wah-wah or fuzz or any sort of extreme distortion. Nor could I stand the endless soloing of guitarists like Eric Clapton or Jimi Hendrix – to me they just sounded like noise. This was a constant worry to me that nagged away at my young conscience ceaselessly. I began to think there was something seriously wrong with me. All my friends seemed to like it and raved on and on about the Groundhog's 'Split' and Rory Gallagher, but I just didn't get it. Being a tunes man, myself, I couldn't rationalise the unfettered, almost undisciplined racket with any sort of tune. Of course, that was where I was going wrong as soloing depended upon improvisation and flair, not rigid rules, but there didn't seem to be anything out there that could help bridge the gap. What was much, much worse was that in this respect, I actually agreed with my parents who also hated loud guitars and I didn't like the feeling one bit. This was youth culture and as a youth I ought to like it in defiance of my parents' generation.

Thankfully, relief finally arrived the day I heard and subsequently purchased, Chicago's '25 or 6 to 4'.

'Chicago!?' I hear you cry. 'Weren't they that lot that put out a series of middle of the road ballads in the late 1970s and 1980s?'

And you would be right because they were. But you would also be half informed because for a short period around 1969–1971, Chicago was a hugely energetic and inventive jazz/rock band of epic proportions. Of their seven members, three sang, nearly all of them wrote and they all played a variety of instruments with consummate skill. Their guitarist, Terry Kath, was the man who showed me that guitar solos could be fun.

The single that I originally heard is actually an edited version of an LP track which gives full rein to Kath's irrepressible guitar, but it was a start and it prompted purchase of the double album from whence it came as soon as funds were available. The song starts with a classic guitar riff and already the stage is set. A tricky brass arrangement leads into the first verse sung by a very young sounding Peter Cetera and at the end of the verse, Kath's guitar sets out its stall with a beautifully liquid run into the second verse – an omen of what is to come. By the end of verse two, being unable to wait a moment longer, Kath takes the song by the scruff of the neck and stamps his guitar all over it in emphatic style. But, and here's the thing, it's not a load of directionless noise, it's wondrously melodic, skipping up and down scales with fluid dexterity. In addition, the solo has structure and is divided into sections, each one adding to the drama as it builds to a stunning climax. Each section uses a different electronic effect, including the dreaded wah-wah pedal, and is played on a different part of the guitar fretboard to emphasise the difference in both tone and pitch. It is truly masterful in its conception and execution and to this day remains my favourite guitar solo ever. There is an exuberance to his playing on this track that manifests itself in the remaining verses where, riffs and fills tumble out around the vocal lines. Like a playful puppy with a bone, he just can't seem to let it go. Finally, I understood. I knew what it was all about and went back to the likes of Clapton and Hendrix with a new outlook and fell in love with guitars. In fact, if I have a criticism of today's bands it is that they avoid the guitar solo like the plague. Perhaps they fear the stigma of being labelled self-indulgent, but I think this is sad. It seems to reflect either a lack of adventure in today's music or the imposition of some form of musical political correctness, but a well-constructed solo is part of the lifeblood of rock and should never be out of fashion. Rather unexpectedly, the last live music I heard to use a proper guitar solo in the set was the rock meets gay disco of the glamorous Scissor Sisters and they did it with some aplomb. Like some rare exotic plant, it is heartening to see that the solo survives in the most unlikely places. Long may it continue to do so.

All this makes the utter tragedy of Terry Kath's death in 1978 at the age of 31 so poignant (he accidentally shot himself in the head with a gun he believed not to be loaded whilst under the influence of alcohol and drugs – a real rock 'n' roll death if ever there was one). Chicago was never the same band afterwards.

Whilst on the subject of Chicago, the subject of the rock chameleon arises. This is a phenomenon whereby a person that we have known at the start of their career, changes over time, seemingly from one persona to another. As I mentioned, their bass player and singer was Peter Cetera who later had solo hits with 'The Glory of Love', and others in the 1980s. The trouble is that the Cetera that I know is an extremely fine bass player and part-time singer whom I admire greatly. I know most of his bass lines off by heart from countless plays of the first three Chicago double albums (they never did anything by halves – the fourth was a quadruple live album) whilst revising at home for my 'O' Levels. During this period in my life, I had the house to myself during the day and thus the schedule on these occasions went something like:

9.00 am	Get up
9.30 am	Have breakfast
10.00 am	Play 'Chicago 1'
11.00 am	Watch test match with schoolbooks on lap. Revise between balls when the fast bowlers are on. If the spinners are on – forget it.
1.00 pm	Play 'Chicago 2'. Lunch
2.00 pm	Watch test match as before. Play air guitar to '25 or 6 to 4' during tea interval.
6.00 pm	Play 'Chicago 3'. Dinner
7.00 pm	Go out

This seemed to work well and as long as the GCE questions involved Chicago or test cricket, I was laughing.

But the point is; the Peter Cetera in his later guise as purveyor of last-dance-of-the-night ballads is unknown to me. I just don't recognise him as the same person. And this seems to happen to me frequently. Another good example is Phil Collins. To me, he is the endlessly inventive drummer with Genesis, who, in the seventies produced a string of classically English progressive albums. The media friendly, singer songwriter Phil of later years doesn't seem to relate to my image of him at all. Perhaps this is a manifestation of that part of the British psyche that dismisses success as a gimmick – and let's be honest, both Collins and Cetera have been successful artists in the music world attaining international solo recognition. It's almost as if we wish fervently that they don't have anything resembling a career. However, on thoughtful reflection, I think it more likely that we never really want our heroes to grow up and expand their horizons because it dismantles our own cosy image of them at a time when we, too, were part of their lives, albeit vicariously. It makes us look at ourselves in a way that perhaps we are not yet ready to do. Certainly, it forces us to admit that time has passed and we have become older, and for most of us, distinctly less successful than our heroes. But also it reminds us of a time when we were more easily enthused, less cynical and perhaps more easily pleased and it's a place that we can no longer visit with ease.

Chapter Four

LISTEN TO THE MUSIC

There's a track on Dire Straits' eponymous first album (the good one) called 'Six Blade Knife' that needs very careful attention. It glides along in moderately paced common time propelled by Pick Withers' brushed snare drum and John Illsley's simple bass line and is punctuated by Mark Knopfler's Dylan meets Tom Waites vocal lines and stabs of solo guitar. The mix of this track has de-emphasised the rhythm section and made the guitar licks much louder by comparison. This creates a dynamic tension between the rhythm section and the guitar lines – a trick used all the time in later Dire Straits songs. The lack of any rhythm guitar or keyboards means that the underlying harmony of the song is carried in the bass line only, or so it seems. But if you listen very carefully, you can just make out David Knopfler's strummed rhythm guitar adding colour to the chord structure. It is very, very faint, almost as if he has turned his amplifier down to the absolute minimum, but it is there nevertheless. In fact, when the main guitar solo starts you can hear…

'So, what's your view on that then, Martin?'

'Err, sorry, what are we talking about?'

Yes, I've been caught out again. I've fallen into the embarrassing trap of listening to the background music at a dinner party, rather than following the conversation. This used to happen all the time, until I stopped receiving invitations to such events. It is a major problem for us music obsessives, we just can't help listening to music and it doesn't really matter where we are, nor in what circumstances.

But the real question is; why do we play music and then talk over it as if it wasn't there? What is the point of playing a CD at a gathering of friends when no one is supposed to listen to it? There doesn't seem to be any rule of social etiquette that covers this sort of thing. Yet, to me it seems disrespectful to talk over something that artists, musicians, producers and studio staff have sweated blood to produce. Just as great works of fiction deserve to be read, rather than bought in order to sit on a shelf as an indication of intellectual prowess, so music deserves to be listened to rather than talked over. It also makes the decision as to what to play at these sorts of social gatherings so much harder. Does one play the sort of stuff that you, as host, like, or do you pander to the tastes of your guests? And does it really matter, as everyone will talk over it anyway? I once knew someone who would cut through all this social nicety by bringing his own music with him, removing the host's choice and then playing his stuff to anyone who would listen. This applied to home visits, car journeys and any other opportunity for music to be played and who is to say that this is not the correct approach?

The absence of rules also affects all public places, hotels, restaurants, shops and airports. Do artists really create art (for that is what it is, despite what you may think from time to time) so that it can be forced upon people, such as when they take a ride in a lift, or studiously ignored, such as in a restaurant? Somehow, I just can't just see Roger Waters and Dave Gilmour sitting down to write 'Dark Side of the Moon' and thinking: 'this will be ideal for playing in the toilets at Gatwick Airport'.

Brian Eno, perhaps, but not Roger and Dave.

One of my more recent CD purchases has been 'Is This It?' by the Strokes. Track seven is called 'Last Nite' and it is fairly representative of the album as a whole in that it belts along at a fair pace with noisy guitars, pounding drums and thumping bass underpinning Justin Casablanca's gravely growl.

The last time I heard this track was in my local Superdrug store where I was the only customer except for an aged woman who was trying to work out how far her pension would stretch. I can't imagine that a blast of the Strokes was actually improving her shopping experience and quite frankly it wasn't helping mine either. The piping of music into the store in this instance was quite pointless and may even have helped reduce the turnover of the shop by irritating its customers beyond endurance, so why do it? It also angers me that someone else has decided when and where I should listen to music. If I am to pay the sort of attention that music deserves, then it should be my decision as to when I am ready and able to give that attention. We live in a noisy world. Anyone who has tried to listen to a personal music player out of doors will know that noise from road traffic, trains, aircraft, construction works and a host of other sources is constantly intrusive. What we don't need is unnecessary music to add to the din.

I read somewhere that the advent of background music in every walk of life coincides with society's fear of silence. The theory goes that no one can bear not to hear a continuous noise in case they are forced to think. Makes you think, doesn't it?

In what must be the ultimate background music situation, many people will claim, in a glow of nostalgia, that they first made love listening to 'Tubular Bells' or whatever it happened to be at the time, and I'm sure they are being honest in their assertions. The only question I would ask is, 'How did you fight the urge to stop what you were doing after 10 minutes and say, "There's a really good bit coming up..."?' Somehow, I just can't see it.

Don't imagine that I used to spend all my time at dinner parties ignoring people and secretly listening to whatever it was playing on their stereo. Oh no, there's secretly having a peek at your host's record/CD collection as well. To the seasoned peeker, this can tell you all sorts of things about a person. For starters, a person's age can be reasonably judged by the volume of recordings bought in certain years. Usually, this will indicate the years when that person was aged between about 15 and 25. After that most people become distracted by work, marriage and children, hence the purchases thin out. Be warned that this sort of age guessing can lead to horrendous social gaffes if your subject was inexplicably interested in say, Mississippi Delta Blues at an early age. Judging age from these clues may result in banishment from your social circle, especially if it's a woman.

The general rule is that most people are not collectors in the accepted sense, but this makes it all the more fascinating. There are always surprises in store. I once knew a girl whose collection you could count on the digits of one hand and four of them were typically what you would expect to find – Fleetwood Mac, Phil Collins, Elton John and Billy Joel. The fifth one was 'Mental Notes' by Split Enz – they of the Harlequin costumes and painted faces. The copy she possessed was a UK based re-recording of the Enz original Australian debut, produced by Phil Manzanera of Roxy Music and is one of my all time favourite albums. But, mainstream it is not. This is an album written by Phil Judd and Tim Finn (before the arrival of Neil Finn) and is the loopiest mixture of rock, avant-garde jazz, music hall whimsy and antipodean folk you could ever wish to hear. Each song is crammed to bursting with musical ideas that swirl around in a maelstrom of sound without any sort of regard for things like key, tempo or rhythm and on first hearing is rather disconcerting. You are as likely to hear a bit of blistering rock guitar, as you are a spoons solo (really). Quite how this album got together with the others, I am at a loss to explain. But this is the joy of checking out other peoples' collections and has nothing to do with being nosey. Honest.

The other side of the coin is that you may also find one of those rash purchases that we all make, lurking in a collection of otherwise exemplary credibility. These are the snippets of knowledge that are always useful when a bit of blackmail is needed to say, secure a lift to the station when it is raining. Just mention that certain Bay City Rollers album, or anything by Rick Wakeman, lurking in the poor unfortunate's collection and the deal's done.

Albums are all very well, but if you really want to get under the skin of your chosen victim, you need to get access to their *singles* collection as it is here that you will find the real embarrassments. Singles are, or certainly were, so much less expensive than albums and are therefore a more spontaneous and ultimately throwaway acquisition. Most people buy singles on a whim. There's none of the weeks of agonising, picking it up in record shops and then putting it back, trying to listen to it first and so on that goes into album purchases. A single is bought in a moment and then usually regretted at length. That is why everyone has at least a few real toe curlers in their collection. I'm surprised that politicians don't head straight for the singles collection when trying to dig the dirt on members of the opposition. You can imagine the scene:

A darkened room in a mock Tudor country retreat. The window is open and two shadowy figures armed with torches are rifling the drawers of a vast mahogany desk.

'Found anything yet?'

'No. Not a sausage. You?'

'No. Only some papers referring to some big financial fraud or other. There's some letters from what looks like a past mistress, but I just binned those.'

'Wait! I've found something. Yes! I think we've hit pay dirt. An old Christmas number one from St Winifred's School Choir, Rolf Harris 'Two Little Boys' and, yes, this is the clincher, 'Unchained Melody' by Robson & Jerome.'

'Bloody Hell! The bastard! Quick, package them up. We're out of here.'

Just on the off chance that in the far distant future anyone reading this is ever invited to my house and intends to embarrass me by raiding my own singles collection, I submit here, for your enjoyment and in order to pre-empt any unpleasantness, my own 'Top Five Singles of Shame':

1. Ding-a-Dong – Teach In.

Well, what can I say? Those of you with long memories will remember that this was the Netherlands' winning entry in the Eurovision Song Contest in 1975. This was also the year that the British entry came eighth and was sung by that well-known vocal combo: The Shadows. This was one of those occasions where my in-built sixth sense for quality new bands came a dreadful cropper. This was a speculative purchase, bought on the assumption that Teach In would become a reasonably major force in the music world and that I would then be able to boast idly, in a superior sort of way, that I had bought all their early singles before they were well known. There had been a precedent set and it was Abba's win the year before with 'Waterloo' which, not surprisingly, sounds somewhat like 'Ding-a-Dong'. My relationship with Abba has been a strange one. I really didn't like the Euro style tweeness of 'Waterloo' and still don't. Nor did I like 'Ring Ring', their re-release of the previous year's failed Eurovision entry, or even 'I Do, I Do, I Do, I Do, I Do', the subsequent single and by this time I had dismissed them as a rather quaint glam rock outfit and filed them under 'ignore'. But then came a road to Damascus moment when I first heard S.O.S. and everything changed. It dawned on me that those who label Abba as a happy-go-lucky band who churn out sing along pop tunes are rather missing the point. All the best Abba songs, and S.O.S. is one of them, comprise a lyrical tragedy of Shakespearean proportions set, rather oddly, to a truly uplifting tune – a sort of trial and redemption in one package. In this instance we have the statutory tragic story of lost love which, remember, was written in a foreign language as far as Bjorn is concerned. Musically, Benny starts the verse in a beautifully melancholic minor key which toggles back and forth onto a suspended seventh chord giving a wistful feel to the lyric. This segments into an alternating major then minor key bridge passage, culminating in an inspired chorus, which ends on a repeated phrase over a rush of ascending major chords. It's the sort of thing J S Bach would have dashed off before lunch. The whole thing is seamlessly constructed and it convinced me that these guys knew how to write great pop songs. I was living in a Hall of Residence at University at the time S.O.S. was released and I used to play it every morning before breakfast to set me up for the day, much to the annoyance of the post grad who occupied the adjoining room. He came round to tell me so on several occasions. However, Abba, a bit like The Carpenters before them, trod a dangerously shaky tightrope between magnificence and toe curling embarrassment. So although I subsequently bought every Abba single thereafter, they sorely tried my resolve with stuff like 'I Have a Dream' and 'Thank You for the Music'. Anyway, I had high hopes for Teach In, who at the time seemed possibly in the Abba mould and that's the case for the defence, m'lud. Recently, there has been some late evidence provided by Bristol University's physiologist and music expert Dr Harry Witchel who has proposed that winning tunes at the song contest have to have seven crucial elements to them. These include attributes such as pace and rhythm, an easily memorable song, a perfect chorus, a key change, and a clearly defined finish. On this basis he cites Abba's 'Waterloo' as the best example but at number four in his list is no less than 'Ding-a-Dong'.

2. My Man and Me – Lynsey De Paul.

In the early 1970s, the singer songwriter came of age. In the 1950s and 1960s songs were usually written by songwriters and performed by performers. There was a tradition, especially in America for the formation of music businesses where songwriters were herded into small bare rooms with a piano to bash out hits all day every day for others to perform. The infamous Brill Building in Broadway, New York is the usual example of this type of undertaking. Both Carole King and Neil Sedaka worked there. Bob Dylan and The Beatles changed all that in that they were writers *and* performers and so were born the singer songwriters. In the 1970s there were masses of them (and mostly ex-Brill Building inmates) – Neil Diamond, James Taylor, Neil Young, Paul Simon and Don McLean and on the distaff side there was Joni Mitchell, Joan Baez, Carole King (now performing her own work) and Laura Nyro amongst many others. The problem with all this talent was that it becomes more difficult to differentiate the great from the good. Enter, Lynsey De Paul, singer songwriter. She had had a reasonable debut hit with 'Sugar Me' in 1972, but by 1975 when this single was released, the cupboard was a little bare. This sub-Bacharach ballad complete with muted brass is really only suited to the cabaret circuit. Still, I was probably in love with her at the time and it could have been worse. It could have been that dreadful 'Rock Bottom' duet with Mike Moran.

3. Madhouse Rag – Mike Batt.

I have to confess that I don't even remember buying this. Nor can I imagine why I should have done. After all, Mike Batt was not only the man in the Womble suit, but also the producer responsible for reducing one of my favourite bands, Steeleye Span, from a genuinely innovative folk/rock fusion band to that which released 'All Around My Hat'. So this one's a bit of a mystery. I'd like to think that I was the victim of a prank, whereby I was drugged and then taken to a record shop and chained to this single like a groom on his stag night, but it doesn't seem very likely. On listening to it again, (and I did have to listen to it again as I couldn't remember it) the mystery deepens. Why did I buy this piece of second-rate ELO pastiche – it didn't even trouble the charts?

4. Also Sprach Zarathustra – Deodato

This is a perfect example of the dangers of buying songs that are playing in a shop whilst you browse. In this case all it has proved is that Deodato makes good browsing music, but in the cold light of a home stereo it immediately transforms itself into a load of pretentious noodling dressed up as 'modern' take on the famous film score. Generally, I have resisted buying music that is playing in music shops but somehow this one seemed different. Being in a relaxed, anticipatory I'm-just-about-to-buy-another-record frame of mind does tend to blind you to the knowledge that it is bound to turn out badly. Anyway, I bought it and it did. I really must be a glutton for punishment, as even this hasn't stopped me trying. Recently, in a well-known London music store, I found myself listening to a rather beautiful track comprising a haunting female vocal over a sparse, rather arid musical backdrop. Not recognising it, I went to the information desk and inquired as to what it was. The two assistants thought for a bit then decided they didn't know either (that's why they work there). Nevertheless, one took it upon himself to ring the DJ on their internal phone system and find out. The answer duly obtained, he rushed round the aisles and returned with a CD, which I then purchased. On hearing it at home it became apparent that this was not what I had heard at all. The male vocalist gave it away. I returned it, got my money back and I still don't know what it was. The only instance where this in-shop buying impulse has worked for me was when I was encouraged to buy a self-titled album by Jane Aire and the Belvederes in 1979. This is a gem of a record that is sadly, long since deleted and currently unavailable on CD. It makes you wonder about the criteria used when deciding which albums should be re-released in new formats when albums of this quality are passed over.

5. They Don't Know – Tracey Ullman

I'm including this at number five not because it's a poor single, but because I bought the wrong version. Of course, what should really be sitting in my singles collection is the late Kirsty MacColl's original version, but unfortunately, as far as I know, it was never released as a single and I never got around to buying the album from which it comes, hence

Tracey Ullman. In fact this is a superb song, written by a master songwriter. It's one of those cases where a great lyric meets a great tune and produces a song that you seem to know on first hearing and then can't forget. There is a real fluidity to the melody which is enhanced by the way the phrasing of the lyrics crosses musical sections as evidenced by the way that the first line linking verse to chorus starts halfway through the preceding verse forcing the singer either to have the lung capacity of an elephant, or to breathe awkwardly in the middle of the phrase.

'And I don't (big breath) listen to the guys who say…'

Great fun for karaoke singers. Tracey doesn't make a bad job of it, but this is Kirsty's song and it should be her singing it.

So, there you have it, five classic examples of how anyone can go seriously wrong without even trying. There are one or two more that I'm not particularly proud of but I think that covers the worst of the blackmail material. As you see, it can happen to the best of us so my only advice is: don't go into politics or any public office if you value your singles collection.

In our modern technological age, there is no reason to leave CD singles lying around as all songs can be downloaded from the Internet and then hidden away on computers and MP3 players and so we may cover our tracks, as it were, but there was something to be said for the old vinyl 7-inchers in that they proclaimed our choices and we stood by our decisions in the face of ridicule. Character building, it used to be called.

Chapter Five

ON THE THRESHOLD OF A DREAM

There are certain points in your life that you look back on and recognise as a defining moment. Such a moment occurred in bed, late one night in 1971 and it's not what you're thinking. Listening to the pirate station Radio Caroline on a small medium-wave transistor radio via an earpiece was a dodgy business in those days as the reception wavered backwards and forwards between teeth-gritting static and sudden bell like clarity like a drunk in a storm. Suddenly, after a particularly nasty burst of static, part of a song emerged for probably thirty seconds or so and then vanished into the ether. This brief annoyance had occurred countless times before and I could have ignored it and moved on. But this had awakened my interest and the damage had been done. A door had been kicked open to a brave new world and I could never go back. Much as I might try to deny it, this was the third and final key point in the life cycle of the bug and I was lost to music forever.

There was no avoiding the issue; this song segment had been a revelation. It comprised two weird intertwining, synthesised riffs over a stately yet energetic drum pattern overlaid with rippling guitar fills and what sounded suspiciously like a violin. On top of it all was this serene female vocal line carrying a strangely accented melody, through at least two changes of tempo. The problem was; I didn't know what it was called, or whom it was by, as the DJ had been submerged in static. But I had to know and there followed a frantic period, during which time I listened at every opportunity to every radio station I could in the hope of hearing it again. Days passed and there was no clue to its identity. I began to think that I wouldn't remember it even if I heard it again as the memory dimmed over time. And then it happened. It was played on a chart rundown one Sunday afternoon and I knew its identity at last. It was 'Back Street Luv' by a band called Curved Air.

Up until this juncture I had been what you might call a singles chart follower. I knew every top twenty chart entry since that day in 1963 when 'She Loves You' burst into my consciousness, but now I had been shown the way to a new and more exciting world – the world of the album. Even though 'Back Street Luv' was a single release, I threw caution to the wind and bought Curved Air's 'Second Album' as it was imaginatively titled and was amazed at its content: haunting melodies, strange instrumental arrangements and at the close of side two, a twelve minute 'song' called 'Piece of Mind' divided into several different musical sections and containing unusual lyrics, including a spoken part of T.S. Eliot's poem 'The Waste Land' although I didn't recognise it as such at the time. Pretentious? Probably, but it was certainly different and to a boy brought up on chart hits, very enticing. This discovery broke the mould of singles fascination for three main reasons:

1. I had been used to hearing standard chart fare where the band's constituents generally conformed to the standard guitar, bass and drums (plus or minus keyboards) configuration of your average rock band. Curved Air, by contrast, had opted for a drums, bass, violin and synthesiser line-up, with occasional guitar ready on the subs bench. In 1971 the synthesiser was a very new instrument indeed and the electric violin was not exactly standard either. Together, they injected an array of previously unheard sounds into popular music. The no guitar option was a bit scary, but only seemed to add to the attraction. Curved Air had a sound that was unique to them and it raised them from the sea of conformists. Like most unusual forms, it wasn't long before their line-up

reverted to a more conventional configuration, but for a few years in the early 1970s, they were different.

2. Up until this point, my experience of pop songs was the three-minute single constructed in a largely standard format. In Curved Air, the two main writers in the band, Daryl Way and Francis Monkman were classically trained and didn't feel the need to be constrained by accepted songwriting structures, or rhythms or anything else come to that. Whilst this trait may not necessarily be classified as desirable, it was certainly different and it opened my ears to more adventurous forms.

3. They were led by a female singer, Sonja Kristina, who was not only the owner of that serene voice, but at a time when the rock world was not swarming with style gurus and image consultants, also looked good in a hippyish sort of way. I found her demeanour of almost detached intensity intriguing and the combination of her voice and the construction of the band as a whole, very attractive. Little did I know at the time that this was to lead to a lifelong penchant for female vocalists in bands.

In short, so-called 'progressive rock' had arrived in my life. In the history of popular music, progressive rock has probably had the worst press imaginable and for one good reason: it lost its way, big time. A bit like Frankenstein's monster, it started out as a good idea, but then it got out of control and started killing people in the woods. But, for a period in the late sixties and early seventies, progressive rock was no more than the next logical step forward, following on from the lead of Bob Dylan's lyrical invention and the Beatles' musical experimentation in the mid 1960s. Bands such as Pink Floyd, King Crimson, Soft Machine and their ilk had taken the whimsy out of psychedelia and were pushing the boundaries to see what would happen in the same way that the bands of the 1960s beat boom had done. Yes, Genesis, ELP, Gentle Giant, Caravan and others followed and for a time some very interesting music was made. It was the sort of music that would have current corporate music executives running for cover in this ever more materialistic world where only the more commercial succeed. Everything was a legitimate target for change, song structures, song length, time signatures, key, use of classical instrumentation and so on. The musicians pleased themselves and the fans listened earnestly. However, by the mid 1970s it had all gone a bit pear-shaped as the isolating influence of success coupled with a dearth of new ideas led to introspective indulgence, but to tar all progressive rock with the brush of failed experiments, is denying the reality that rock was changed forever by the ideas produced by this genre. The likes of Radiohead, Muse and even Coldplay are really only today's descendants of this musical form and it hasn't done them any harm.

Finding the key to the world of albums was all very well, but discovering which new bands I would like and consequently follow was a little more complicated than I had anticipated. By the end of the sixties, the music market had divided into two camps: those that released a steady stream of singles and appeared on TOTP and those that, perhaps rather pompously, only released albums, like Led Zeppelin and Pink Floyd (post Syd Barrett). One or two did both, such as Jethro Tull, but they were in the minority. I already knew about the first category, having followed the charts for many years, but the second category required a tad more research. There were several sources of information, one of which was to listen to the very small number of radio programmes that featured the new progressive bands, such as John Peel's BBC Radio 1 show or even Alan Freeman's Saturday afternoon slot.

Another source of information was to read the music press and so I became an avid reader of the *Record Mirror*, having discovered it in my local newsagent. Up until then, I had been completely oblivious to the existence of music papers but having made the discovery, was astounded to find all sorts of useful trivia and better still, pictures of my idols looking scruffy and rebellious. It is difficult to imagine now, from a distance of thirty years, how ungroomed pop stars were then. It speaks of an age where musicians made music, not image conscious wannabes with a corporate expense account. At that time there were a plethora of music weeklies available; *Melody Maker*, *Sounds and New Musical Express*, or NME, as it is known, in addition to *Record Mirror*. Sadly, all these publications have vanished with the exception of NME, which just goes to show how the importance of music has diminished for today's youth. After a year or two I shifted my allegiance to *Sounds* and eventually to the NME with its fiendishly difficult crossword. In fact, I have only just given up buying it, mainly through embarrassment, but probably because I can no longer do the crossword – it just doesn't seem right for a middle-aged man to be reading such a youth orientated publication and in recent times I had been fighting the urge to hide it amongst other magazines at the shop counter in an distinctly furtive manner, so it had to go. As an aside, it is interesting to note how many well-known people started out writing for the NME. Amongst those early scribblers at the NME offices there are those that have graduated to broader based writing such as Julie Birchill and Tony Parsons, those that now appear regularly as talking heads on television such as Andrew Collins and Stuart Maconie and those that entered the music business proper like DJ Steve Lamacq and artists such as Bob Geldof, Neil Tennant and Chrissie Hynde. All of which helps to prove that music obsessives can still turn out to be reasonably useful members of society.

A third source of music education was clubs and discos, but this experience tended to occur by default rather than being actively sought. I generally shied away from discos as this involved dancing, a thing to be avoided at all costs but occasions did arise where my school friend, John would drag me along in order to meet girls. The irony here was that John had no difficulty meeting girls at any time, and didn't really need to go to discos to do it. Having the dark chiselled looks of a young Bryan Ferry, he was seemingly irresistible to women and on our few ventures to discos would usually pick someone up within the first few minutes leaving me to while away the rest of the evening alone. Nevertheless, these were times when I could listen to what was being played and in the days when discos offered mainly chart material and oldies rather than the sort of specialised ambient club music today's youth is subjected to, this meant a few hours at the bar soaking up the ear shatteringly loud sounds for future reference.

The final source of information was by word of mouth. By this time I had moved on to an all boys secondary school, a 1930s collection of forbidding red brick buildings with green stained clock tower, near the centre of St Albans and word of mouth meant discussing trends with my fellow pupils during those idle moments, like morning break and double physics. This was when I made a disconcerting discovery. To say that children are cruel is but an inconsequential nothing compared to adolescents when discussing popular music. Lifelong friendships could be made or broken dependent upon the agreement or otherwise that, say, 'Caroline' by Status Quo was any good and any slight indication that you were leaning the wrong way and the deep well of unpopularity beckoned. In the alien environment that was the school playground, factions would form and sides were taken. In the days before computer games, mobile phones, DVD players and a multitude of other distractions, the only thing worth getting worked up about was music and my generation got very worked up about it indeed.

As an illustration of just how serious the youth of my day took their musical education, I recount the following story. When I had reached the sixth form, those of us who had the responsibility of prefectdom thrust upon us were charged with running our own detention classes, after school hours. This generally required that the unfortunate inmates copy out texts for half an hour as a time-wasting exercise, to the general boredom of all concerned. On one occasion, fired by a desire to make it a tad more interesting and in a fit of inspiration, a fellow prefect tasked his detention attendees with writing a review of their most recently purchased LP, rather than copy out from the dog-eared books we supplied. Presumably, out of grateful relief, all of them turned in a decent attempt and we all had a good laugh reading them afterwards. I doubt you would get the same commitment today from a selection of young troublemakers.

Entry into music discussions was initially a scary and intense undertaking and it took a certain amount of courage to join in but after a period of nerveless bluff and genuine interest, it would soon become apparent that any newcomer was either worth his salt or a hopeless case. Once you were accepted as a fellow rock bore, discussions took on a less argumentative tone and became a bit more productive. Eventually, talk would lead to curiosity and curiosity to borrowing and borrowing to having to carry the damn thing around all day before taking it home. Thus were born what were termed the 'Carriers'; that is, those albums that were the most popular to be seen carrying around school, in the manner of a fashion accessory, without sending your carefully constructed façade as rock critic into a nosedive. The problem with 12-inch vinyl was that it was very difficult to hide due to its size. Therefore, no one could be seen with any album that didn't cut the mustard. At around the time I am describing, the top three carriers, as sported by those in the know, were:

1.   In the Court of the Crimson King – King Crimson

You may know this one. It's the cover with the startling pink and mauve painting of a face with mouth open and nostrils flared giving the viewer a graphic look at teeth, tonsils and other rather unsavoury anatomical bits. This album lays claim to being the first ever progressive rock record, containing as it does, masses of moody mellotron, long structured pieces, rather than songs, and weird fairytale lyrics. It is almost wilfully unorthodox, being, according to its creators, not an LP record but an 'observation' by King Crimson. Blimey. With all this weirdness going on from cover to content, this was a heaven sent Carrier album, being universally acknowledged as a genuinely baffling, highbrow product and with a cover that you could spot a mile off thus advertising your good taste. Funny to think that the main instigator of this oddness, Robert Fripp, is now married to Toyah.

2.   Five Bridges – The Nice

The Nice vied with King Crimson for the title of first ever progressive band, their respective album contenders being released within a month or so of each other in 1969. This one was their fourth effort and shows an arty, kaleidoscopic view of a suspension bridge on the cover. The Nice's line-up included one Keith Emerson who would team up with Greg Lake from King Crimson and Carl Palmer to form the infamous Emerson, Lake and Palmer, perhaps one of the main reasons why progressive rock got such a bad name. Many progressive bands borrowed classical music structures, but the Nice seemed to go one step further by actually playing interpretations of classical pieces, as in this album and extracts from Musicals such as 'America' from West Side Story. This was a good solid Carrier favoured by those doing 'A' level music but not really in the same class as King Crimson.

3.   Umma Gumma – Pink Floyd

Another schoolboy intellectual classic with a too-clever-by-half cover depicting a picture within a picture within a picture in pseudo Escher style where the four members of the band change positions in each picture. This is the Pink Floyd at their most experimental (or most unlistenable, depending on your view) and comprises a double album where the first record essays lengthy live interpretations of earlier works and the second record contains ten minutes or so of individual experimentation from each of the four members of the band. Interesting is probably the adjective you would use to describe this adventure although Roger Waters's 'Granchester Meadows' is a beautifully evocative piece of acoustic guitar, voice and summer sound effects (bees, songbirds etc.) on tape loops that seems strangely traditional amongst the other more radical pieces. Again, this was a reliable Carrier and quite adequate if you needed to parade your credentials but didn't have access to either of the other two.

Whilst these albums were in general circulation, it was wise not to attempt any other lending for fear of ridicule, but there were alternative avenues open to exploitation. My own solution to the problem of LP Carriers was to introduce an album that nobody else knew anything about, thereby wrong footing those waiting to pounce with withering remarks and sidestepping any serious criticism. One Saturday, whilst listening to the radio in the summer of 1972, I had heard a track called 'Borrowed Time' by an American all girl quartet called Fanny. The song not being a single release, I purchased 'Fanny Hill', the album from which it came and found that I liked it a lot. Fanny was a genuinely pioneering rock band. Bear in mind that, up until this point, there had never been any female rock bands that wrote, sang and played their own material and you will appreciate that Fanny was up against an appalling amount of male chauvinism. Nevertheless, they resisted the condescension from both the press and the music industry, and stayed around long enough to release four well received albums on Reprise records before imploding. Their lasting legacy is the firm foundation they laid for the likes of the Go-Gos and the Bangles that followed.

Thus stimulated, I subsequently bought 'Charity Ball' their previous effort, but was a little agitated to discover that their eponymous debut was not available in the UK. I therefore contacted an import shop via an advertisement in the NME and, after several weeks' breathless waiting, a copy was duly secured for me direct from the USA. It then occurred to me that this was the perfect Carrier LP with which to amaze my friends. Luckily, within my own circle of friends, only I knew of Fanny, or anything about them and their America only debut release debarred anyone from getting hold of it without a struggle. Clearly, I was in a win win situation and as predicted, it held me in good stead for at least a term and a half. No one dare ask what it was without immediately revealing themself as a charlatan of the worst sort. For example:

'Sir, what have you there?'

'Upon my soul, have you not heard of the latest popular combo, Fanny?'

(Thinks: Gadzooks! Search me!) 'Err... of course my good sir, what do'est thou take me for?'

(In order to avoid legal obscenity complications, I leave the reader to translate into sixteen-year-old schoolboy vernacular as required.)

Inevitably, this led to a flurry of ever more obscure albums doing the rounds as competition for exclusivity grew to outrageous proportions and helps to explain why artists such as that purveyor of perversely difficult jazz rock, Henry Cow, took on such cult status amongst certain of my classmates. In the great scheme of things, all this diversity was undoubtedly a good thing and helped to reveal gems like 'White Bird' from the oddly named Californian band, It's a Beautiful Day and the classical rock of 'Kings and Queens' from the initial incarnation of Renaissance. It is a period that I look back on with some fondness, linked as it is with discovery and inspiration and it is one that provides many of the albums I still like to indulge today. What is also true, however, is that it is probably neither better nor worse than any other period in the last fifty years (except perhaps the mid 1970s) but it is the time when musical perception was widened and the excitement of its potential was a driving force in my life. It is almost impossible to maintain that level of awe as the years pass and the accumulation of experience renders most 'new' music to be falsely innovative and rooted in the past.

No doubt in the perception of my elders, this also applies to my own period of awakening but for me, without the consciousness of its history, music could be enjoyed for its own merit alone. Sadly, this is a situation that becomes more difficult to achieve with the wider exposure that the passing of time brings. I find that virtually everything sounds like something else and only the very extreme experiments can be classified as genuinely new and this is a shame. I can only hope that pop music does not tread the same path of atonality and avant-garde experimentation that marred classical music in the first half of the twentieth century and almost brought it to its knees. Thus far, this has not happened and I hope that the endless ability for rock to reinvent itself will continue to thrive for the benefit of future generations.

Chapter Six

MONEY FOR NOTHING

Whilst the form of popular music that we know today has only been in existence since the mid twentieth century, I have often mused over whether historic generations have been subjected to the music obsession bug. For example, I have long suspected that Shakespeare must have been a bit of a music obsessive as it was he that wrote the immortal lines:

'Neither a lender nor a borrower be' (Hamlet Act 1, Scene 3) and quite right, too.

He would have understood that vinyl records, unlike today's CDs, were very delicate objects that could become irreparably scratched in an instant if handled incorrectly or not kept in their sleeves. For this reason, no true obsessive likes to lend records to anyone, even friends, and I was no exception. You have to remember that I was the sort of person who would return a record to the shop if the cover was bent or if there was any form of mark or abrasion on the playing surface.

To an obsessive, buying vinyl was an occupation often fraught with frustration and heartbreak and all of it was to do with pressing faults. To arrive home, place your new purchase on the turntable and then listen to a series of clicks, swooshes and crackles was a deeply disheartening experience. This would be compounded by the sure knowledge that the remaining stock in the shop would be in exactly the same condition as most faults ran in batches. Nevertheless, back to the shop it went, usually several times, before you either found a clean copy or, more usually, gave up and accepted a less than perfect copy. Listening for faults on a single LP was bad enough but a faulty double LP could be enough to send you to the funny farm, a gibbering wreck. I only just survived this experience through countless replacement copies of Genesis' 'The Lamb Lies Down on Broadway'. Each new copy had to be listened through carefully before, just when you thought everything was going to be fine (and usually on side four), a brand new fault would become apparent and utter despair would descend. Having listened to the whole double album whilst in an agony of expectation, innumerable times, and without any real enjoyment, I would be bored stiff with the thing by the time I had found a decent copy to play. In this instance to save my sanity, I gave up, accepted my lot and eventually bought a CD copy that is blissfully free of faults. In fact, it sounds a little odd without the clicks and crackles I know so well.

Thus in the days of vinyl, when finding a clean copy was such a trial, lending records was always a bit of a thorny subject, especially when the habits of the borrower were unknown, and a refusal could lead to a cold war of trade embargoes if not handled delicately. For my own part, I would lend only to a select few and then only after exhaustive research into the borrowers' attitudes concerning record handling, absence of sticky fingers, return to sleeves after each play, quality of record playing equipment, returns policy (i.e. was there one?) and a host of other items. Each potential borrower had to satisfy a list of counts that MI5 would have been proud of before they were allowed the privilege of gracing my select list, but it all seemed to work and I had very few casualties through losses or damage. Luckily, the advent of the compact disc has rendered this sort of malarkey redundant, although getting them back from the borrower can still be a problem, but for damage limitation alone the silver discs have earned their keep.

Whilst the problems of faulty records were an occupational hazard for the perennial record buyer, there was always the initial difficulty of finance. Having secured a source of inspiration for future listening from a mixture of peer recommendation and the music press, the impetus for actually getting out there and buying the things was strengthened but my small income only really gave me access to the singles market up until the age of fourteen, give or take the odd Christmas or Birthday present. However a change in fortune was not long coming. During my later school years, I was able to increase my income significantly by obtaining a morning paper round from the local newsagent, at the mouth-wateringly high rate of £1 per week (roughly equivalent to £10 per week now). Although this entailed having to drag myself out of bed at the ungodly hour of 6.30 am, in all weathers for 363 days a year, these riches increased my purchasing power almost beyond imagination to a degree that, potentially, allowed a trip to the Record Room for an LP every two weeks. Notwithstanding the early start, I enjoyed my paper round with its lack of supervision and fresh morning air. It also allowed a period of radio listening with a discrete earpiece – if only the Walkman or the MP3 player had been invented then.

Buying albums was a monumental step up from the one single a month that my pocket money had allowed – and was to prove my undoing. By this time, the music bug had bitten deep and with increased funds at its disposal, I have been forced to continue the trend of buying countless albums for nigh on thirty-five years without respite. It seems that only the advent of a meagre pension can save me now.

The first long-playing record I ever owned was 'Bridge Over Troubled Water' by Simon and Garfunkel and it was given to me as a Christmas present soon after its release. It was an album that I had been itching to hear ever since the success of the title track in the singles chart and it was the first indication of a yearning to investigate artists beyond the one or two songs provided by the singles market. Accordingly, it was not long after that I delved into the uncharted waters of the albums market for the first time and it what an uneasy process it turned out to be.

The first LP record I ever bought with my own money, as opposed to having been given as a present, was Paul

McCartney's first solo effort, recorded at about the time the Beatles were splitting up, entitled simply 'McCartney'. It took me months to buy it as, having been used to dealing in shillings and pence, I had to screw up courage to spend the massive sum of £2 and by the time I had steeled myself to part with my hard earned cash, the purchase had taken on a huge significance. I even went so far as to borrow a copy from a friend first just to make sure that I liked every track on it and would thus not waste a penny of the purchase price. This is laughable now, when I throw away countless pounds on albums I know nothing about only to find that I hate them, but in those more anxious days it was a decision that haunted me for weeks. Finally, the purchase was made and happily, it is still one of my favourite McCartney albums as it has an unforced, home-made feel about it and comprises a mishmash of songs, instrumentals and oddments that were clearly left over from his Beatles days, but have a rather unfinished feel which in my book is preferable to being overproduced. He played all the instruments himself with varying degrees of competence, which again is endearing as it hints that even professional musicians have limits. The following album, 'Ram' is also a collection of differently styled but marginally superior songs and together with the second side of the Beatles' 'Abbey Road', these two albums are probably all you need to know about Paul McCartney at his best.

A couple of years ago, the reissue label, Rhino Handmade, released a boxed set of four CDs containing all Fanny's work for Reprise Records, plus a stack of additional live tracks, demo recordings and unreleased material. One of the extra tracks comprises a rehearsal recording of one of my favourite songs of theirs entitled 'Beside Myself'. This is a smouldering ballad by Nickey Barclay in the style of the Who circa 'Who's Next' and the recording is taken from the very early stages of the song's development. There are a lot of 'la-la-la' vocals where the lyrics have yet to be completed and something goes horribly wrong in the mid section, which the band recovers with some difficulty but the overall effect is magical. They sound loose and relaxed and totally unproduced and all the better for it. Alice deBuhr's drums sound crisp and purposeful and June Millington's guitar is delicate, yet robust. By contrast, the finished song, produced by Todd Rundgren for their 'Mother's Pride' album sounds cold and clinical. It just reinforces my view that less is more when any band or artist has a level of competence that requires no embellishment. Which is why I have an affection for 'McCartney' and any other slightly less than perfect albums.

The promotion to buying albums, rather than singles, not only provided access to artists that shunned single releases but also allowed appreciation of the work of the great and the good. It allowed me to collect work from those artists that frequently appear in lists identifying the biggest global sellers of all time. Thus I have albums by The Beatles, The Beach Boys, Jimi Hendrix, Queen, U2, Madonna, Elton John and so on. Most of these purchases were made on merit and not in order to build a collection comprising the cream of the popular offering, so there was no ulterior motive at work other than enjoyment. But it is most likely that this ad hoc method of collection has, on closer inspection, left some glaring omissions in my collection for which there is no easy excuse. It means that there are some major artists at large in the world that are not represented. The following four are prime examples, for which I will try and formulate an explanation:

1. Bob Dylan

It's not that I don't like Bob Dylan personally or appreciate his place in history; it's just that I've never really been aware of him in the same way that I was aware of, say, The Beatles and thus never got around to buying anything he produced. In his innovative prime in the 1960s, I was probably too young to understand the force of his lyrics and too dazzled by the British beat boom to notice the quality of his music. I often find that there is a kind of unspecified limitation period after which, if no interest has been shown in an artist, it is unlikely that there ever will be and they slip from consciousness. Notwithstanding this effect, even now I find it hard to listen to any of his albums. I have always been aware of a slight nagging that tells me I should own at least one album so I made the decision to pick up a copy of 'Blonde on Blonde' when I espied it in a sale a year or so back, but have only played it once and probably will not do so again unless I am feeling particularly strong. For me, his time has passed. The other disturbing facet is that I tend to prefer other artists' covers of his songs to his originals, which is never a good sign. The time has come to admit that I am quite happy to enjoy his work vicariously through others and not worry about it too much.

2.   David Bowie

Bowie is another inexplicable omission in my collection and all the more mystifying because my brother had copies of 'Hunky Dory' and 'The Man Who Sold the World', which I would borrow constantly and liked a lot and I believe 'A Space Oddity', with its cheap Stylophone solo and lush mellotron setting to be one of the finest singles ever produced. But somehow, the normal progression of buying a few subsequent releases just didn't happen in this case. One reason may well be that at the time of his rise to fame in the early 1970s, I was at school and no one I knew amongst my fellow pupils followed him and therefore he had no profile in our discussions. The effect of peer acceptance in this type of situation is extremely strong and unless an artist has a champion amongst your fellow enthusiasts, the awareness fades very quickly. Even if the artists being championed by various individuals were not to your taste, they remained in the memory and would often be reactivated years later in different conditions. I remember having quite heated arguments with a classmate who championed Steeleye Span, as I despised the very idea of folk music at that time, yet years later found that; actually, I liked their take on modern folk. I wonder if I would have made the effort to persevere if it had not been for the memory of those arguments. But Bowie had no champion and consequently I never really gave him another thought. By way of appeasement, I have bought a 'Best of' collection, which startled me somewhat when I first played it, as it was the later stuff that I found more absorbing than those older tracks that I know so well. And then there's that duet with Mick Jagger, 'Dancing in the Street' which is just so painful to listen to, it requires me to dig out the original version just to confirm that it really was a good song once. I play my compilation from time to time but there is still no spark that will induce me to buy any of his back catalogue.

3.   The Rolling Stones

I can't help thinking that my lack of Stones product really boils down to the old chestnut about the Beatles/Stones divide. Popular belief has it that in the 1960s you were either a Beatles fan or a Stones fan and I was one of the former. To an extent, I was taken in by their 'bad' image of sex, drugs and rock 'n' roll (although the Beatles were no better in this respect) and it tarnished them in my young impressionable mind. Years later, there was a girl I remember at University who would install herself in a corner of the Hall bar. She had adopted a vaguely hippy/gypsy style of clothing and generally wore scruffy jeans and flowery low cut tops which revealed her cleavage and her midriff. With her wild tumbling hair and dark flashing eyes, she oozed sexuality to a quite scary degree and had a disconcerting way of looking at you in a manner that implied she was laughing to herself behind those eyes. Inevitably, she was a huge Stones fan and this only reinforced my perception that they had some connection with the dark side of the force if she was anything to do with it. Despite liking virtually all their singles up to about 'Brown Sugar', their rather doubtful associations were enough to take them outside the limitation period as far as albums were concerned and all was lost. I still own one or two of their singles and a copy of 'Let it Bleed' that is never played, but this is probably as far as I will ever go for them unless I can steel myself to find a 'Best of'. The fact that they are still touring at retirement age is not helping their case either and, increasingly, I find myself being loathe to contribute more cash to the already bloated coffers of Jagger and company.

4. Led Zeppelin

Quite why I failed to buy any Led Zeppelin albums is perhaps a little easier to explain. The solid reason that supports this state of affairs is one of availability. I have never needed to buy any of their albums because I have always been surrounded by them and have been afforded access whenever I chose. Most of my friends at school had copies and later, my newly acquired stepbrothers also brought copies with them. My first year roommate at University had a complete set and would play them at every opportunity. Since then I have never found that I have had the urge to rush out and buy albums that I already know backwards, which is a complete turnaround from those early days when it would be a prerequisite that I knew it backwards before I would even contemplate buying it. As with most of my missing artists, I have eased my conscience by obtaining a 'Best of' collection on CD that gives me as much as I am likely to need and thankfully it doesn't contain the live half-hour version of 'Dazed and Confused' so perhaps I made the right decision after all.

It seems that collecting choices, rather than being based on a grand scheme often hinge on trivial or unrelated conditions like the whims of others or availability or misconstrued perception but it would be expected that with maturity, those choices are rectified – but I wouldn't bank on it. Attitudes, once entrenched and for whatever reason, often endure. Even now, if I hear something by The Sensational Alex Harvey Band or Stackridge, I can hear those long forgotten arguments with school friends resurface and spoil the experience enough for me to ignore them all over again.

In recent years I have tried to fill a few holes in my collection by buying 'classic' albums that I missed the first time around. This exercise has yielded mixed returns and I am gradually coming to the conclusion that the old adage, 'You can't go back' equally applies to old records. If they didn't impress at the time, why should they do so now? There have been one or two successes – 'Surrealistic Pillow' by Jefferson Airplane springs to mind, but generally, like Dylan, Bowie and the Rolling Stones, I have passed beyond.

The inverse of failing to trouble the retailers when it comes to classic rock is the propensity to continue buying the output of a favourite artist, sheep like, well past their sell-by date. In this case a form of aural blindness sets in and it becomes impossible to believe that an artist you have discovered, admired and followed through their golden years has degenerated into a spent force. The sensation is like awakening from a good dream only to find that reality is nothing like the substance of the dream. It took me years of buying every Chicago release up to about Chicago 9 to comprehend that the energetic, inventive band I once knew had become a tired, middle-of-the-road act and worse, that this change in direction had occurred around about volume 6, leaving me with three or four very nondescript albums in my collection. At the time I had genuinely believed that all the albums were of an exacting standard and the shock of realisation was quite severe. A similar experience awaited me with Curved Air, where I studiously bought every recording they put out in every reincarnation of the line-up, but truth be told, only the first three albums with the original line-up are worthy of consideration.

There is something of the mental state of the addict displayed in this type of behaviour in that even after the penny has dropped and we know that we should resist further purchases, our inner obsessive is still yearning to hear any new material in the slight hope that it will be a return to form.

But it rarely is and like the secretive smoker we are left deflated and guilty once more and vowing that we will never do it again – until the next time, anyway. My brother has been buying Robert Plant albums for years, but he has admitted to me that it is not because he enjoys them, it is because he feels he should support an artist he once admired. If that isn't showing all the signs of an obsessive, I don't know what is.

And then there are compilation albums. The first niggle is that many compilations do not run in chronological order and thus destroys any natural story that the band has to tell. On the Pink Floyd's 'Echoes' compilation there is something extraordinarily jarring about hearing the late period 'Learning to Fly' followed by Syd Barrett's 'Arnold Layne' followed by the mid period 'Wish You Were Here' as none of these songs bear any relationship to each other in time or style. For most bands with any longevity their style changes and develops over time. For listeners buying the albums in real time, they live that unfolding story as it happens, but for those who catch up later with a 'Best of' compilation, it would be a shame to withhold the enjoyment of the story even if it is played in fast forward mode. Therefore, it would make sense to run the tracks in time order so that the development of the band becomes apparent and the hearing of it that much more interesting. The Doors' 'Weird Scenes Inside the Goldmine', for example, is not in chronological order and as a consequence, the story of the early extravagantly long pieces, the foolhardy mid period experimentation with orchestras and the final redemption of a return to the Blues is lost amongst the jumble.

This reasoning can also apply to Video collections. The 'Ultimate Kylie' collection of Kylie Minogue's videos is mercifully, correctly ordered from first to last and allows her story to unfold. The first few videos display a young and slightly uncertain Kylie belting out some of Stock, Aitken and Waterman's catchy tunes, but by song number twelve or so, her career is clearly in stagnation as a couple of indifferent covers and more paint by numbers songs illustrate. Suddenly, there is a culture change, as she leaves the paternal set up of S, A & W and arrives at DeConstruction records. The next half dozen videos show her 'rebellion' by engaging in a variety of different styles, some good, some not so good, before the triumphant return as pop princess, starting with 'Spinning Around'.

The second regret associated with compilations is that if you like the band, you inevitably end up buying all their albums anyway so a 'Best of' usually turns out to be costly and redundant, especially if it's a double. But then, what are marketing agencies for?

One final point about albums. Why is it that when I was young and owned the grand total of six vinyl LPs, I had no difficulty in picking one to play, but now that I am confronted with hundreds to choose from, I can never make a choice and often end up doing something else instead? Perhaps someone can tell me.

But we seem to have wandered from the point. What I am trying to say is that I am now, more than ever, convinced that Shakespeare was undoubtedly a fellow sufferer of the music obsession bug. Who else would interrupt a gripping play in mid flow just to give an impromptu critique of some wandering minstrel's verse?

'A hit, a very palpable hit' (Hamlet, Act 5, Scene 2). Mind you, we never found out whether it was, or not.

Chapter Seven

WISH YOU WERE HERE

'Space. The final frontier, blah, blah, blah. Captain's log. Stardate: sometime in the late twentieth century. Subject: Continental Europe. We are in extended orbit around Earth so as not to alarm the inhabitants and have been monitoring radio transmissions from this area of old Earth for some time and have picked up, as yet unidentified bursts of music in three-minute segments.'

'Analysis, Mr Spock?'

'Nothing yet, Captain. We need more data.'

'Speculation, then?'

'As far as I can assimilate, it's rock 'n' roll, Jim. But not as we know it.'

And of course, as usual, he is correct. There is something about popular music that emanates from European countries, other than the UK or even Ireland that is not quite as we would expect it. Anyone who has watched the Eurovision Song Contest will know this to be a fundamental truth. Somewhere along the line they have lost the blueprint and come up with a mutant version that can be original and vital or, more commonly, dreadful. So what is the blueprint and where did it come from? The answer, as we know, is the United States of America and it came in the form of a Blues/Country hybrid from the early pioneers such as Little Richard, Chuck Berry, Fats Domino, Elvis and the rest of the bunch. But, and here's the crunch, it was coded in the English language (well, sort of) and it came early to the UK as part of our traditional trading links with the old colony. When the Beatles were inventing the second wave of the popular music explosion in the early 1960s, they weren't just listening to Tommy Steele and Lonnie Donegan, they were also dashing down to Liverpool docks in a fervour of excitement to see what records had come in with the ships from the States. Imported records from America covered a wide spectrum of styles from black rhythm and blues to white country rock and would have fuelled a melting pot of inspiration for the young greats to be. If you doubt that these white working-class lads were influenced by black Americans, have a listen to Otis Redding's version of 'Daytripper' or Al Green's version of 'I Wanna Hold Your Hand' to see how close to the soul border they were.

It is difficult to imagine someone from Austria or Switzerland dashing to their docks, as a) they didn't have any docks and b) they probably wouldn't be interested in foreign language records even if they did. Then, as now, the UK shares a common language and to a large degree a common culture with America hence the three chord rock 'n' roll format became the standard here as it did there. But not so in Europe. In most European countries, the rock 'n' roll blueprint either came later or not at all and worse still, it came in a foreign language thus making it accessible only to those who had an understanding or those who made the effort. In effect, it arrived after a series of translated Chinese whispers and emerged somewhat altered.

Whether or not all this explains Belgium's Plastic Bertrand of 'Ca Plain Pour Moi' fame, the jury is still out but it certainly pushes a few pointers our way when it comes to explaining why Eurorock, as I shall call it for the purpose of this discussion, is so tantalisingly familiar yet so alien. It is much more likely that Eurorock was initially influenced by traditional folk music of all creeds and the vast heritage of western classical music. Take Dutch band Focus for example. In the 1970s Focus were probably the biggest instrumental band on the planet and had hits with 'Hocus Pocus' and 'Sylvia' but their music is not really based in rock 'n' roll as you might have guessed by the amount of yodelling going on. In fact their big rock number, 'Hocus Pocus' is a musical joke, poking fun at the excesses of rock music as expounded by largely British and American bands. Focus' music is much more aligned with classical styles and forms.

'Sylvia', for example, is very much in the classical style as witnessed by its harmonic movement based on strong descending bass lines and key modulations. J S Bach would have fully understood this piece as it uses all the tools he himself would have used when composing his Italian Concerto that I studied for 'O' Level Music. In addition, many of their extended pieces have a form that is close to classical Sonata Form as used by the great symphonic composers such as Beethoven. In Sonata Form, melodies or themes (usually two) are stated in the exposition section, these themes are then developed or improvised in the development section and finally the themes are restated in the recapitulation. Focus uses this approach in pieces like 'Anonymous' where the middle development section takes the form of a massive extended improvisation exercise by either guitarist Jan Akkerman or keyboard player Thijs van Leer, or both. There are classical motifs in abundance in many of their instrumental pieces from the keyboard arpeggios in 'Focus III' to the fugue in 'Carnival Fugue', both from their sprawling 'Focus 3' double album.

The other major influence in Eurorock is traditional folk music. This is easy to spot and is one of the primary reasons why the Eurovision song contest was so bizarre in the 1960s. During that period, rock 'n' roll was still relatively new to us in Britain, but to someone in Bulgaria or Turkey it was non-existent. This resulted in a contest of modernised folk music, the roots of which are still discernible in today's contests although European music for this purpose has gradually homogenised into a gruesome mixture of old folk and new beats. Abba's music is an example of Eurorock based in traditional folk. Both 'Chiquitita' and 'Take a Chance on Me' have that rather unnerving oompah beat so beloved of German folk bands. Even the Norwegian A-ha, whom you may assume to have thrown off such influences, have a track on their 'Scoundrel Days' album called 'Maybe Maybe' that is dangerously reminiscent of similar folk beats. Generally, there is much to be wary of when checking out European bands, as you can never be sure that the oompah factor will not suddenly surface without warning, so I would recommend caution.

But that is not to say that all Eurorock is second rate because it isn't. In the case of some European bands, it is for the very reason that they have no preconceived ideas about form that there is often an interesting slant placed on tired structures that positively glows with originality. I count A-ha in this category because they produced wildly eccentric versions of rock ballads by using new electronic instruments allied to Morten Harket's exceptionally heroic voice. He is the aural equivalent of the epic Nordic sagas that dominate Scandinavian mythology and can conjure up vast northern wastes with those great rising choruses that A-ha seem to go in for. When the 'Scoundrel Days' album was released in 1986 it became an immediate favourite amongst me and my small band of fellow music lovers and the more I became accustomed to its content through constant playing the more I came to understand that to hear it at its best the listener had to be positioned in an area of outstanding natural beauty, or at least out in the open air. Somehow, indoors on a wet November afternoon just didn't do it.

The first time this became noticeable was during a skiing trip to the French Alps with the aforementioned mates. I had made a tape of the LP so as to listen to it on a Walkman during our time in the mountains and as the week progressed the priority of each day became less to do with the skiing and more to do with who was going to listen to my A-ha tape, to the extent that I had to hide it and sleep with it under my pillow so as to keep it in my possession. The reason why it was so popular was evidently because the big soaring ballads that comprised the majority of the album and Morten Harket's pure, glacial voice became endowed with a life affirming vigour when experienced amongst the snow and vast blue skies of the slopes. In the end, I had to leave the tape behind with the few who were staying on for an extra couple of days and learned later that it had played constantly in their car on the way home through France. I never saw it again.

Music can have this sort of effect and location is everything. I felt it again some time later when returning home on a train from Brighton one summer's eve after a tiring day's work out in the provinces. With my trusty Walkman playing, I lay back in my seat in a deserted carriage and stared through the window as the sun-brightened countryside floated by outside and listened to 'Scoundrel Days'. Again it was the fatal combination of Morten's unique voice and the visions of the English countryside that captured me and took me out of that carriage to somewhere serene and full of contentment. It was a strange and mesmerising experience which only happens once in a while, but which makes listening to music the best occupation there is. Rattling into Waterloo soon put paid to my reverie but for 45 minutes life was a lot of fun.

Now that I come to think about it, there is something quite appealing about Scandinavian bands. Another on the list of favourites is Swedish band The Cardigans, who although now sound pretty much like most other bands, were once much given to quirky arrangements, melt-in-the-mouth melodies and distinctly peculiar song construction. In the mid 1990s their second album 'Life' contained a bunch of songs that sounded at first listen that they had been written around the wrong way in as much as the verse always sounded much better than the chorus. In most songs, the listener tends to put up with the verse in the sure anticipation that a great chorus is only just around the corner, but The Cardigans were having none of that, preferring to give you the best bit first and then follow it up with an averagely predictable chorus. An example would be the song 'Rise and Shine' where you can virtually sing the chorus without even hearing the song but the verse is achingly beautiful and makes 'Rise and

Shine' probably the only song I know where I cannot wait for the chorus to end. Just one more example of what can happen in the world of Eurorock.

One other attribute that the Cardigans have is the ability to arrange their work so that each instrument has a recognisable part that dovetails to the others so that together they produce the whole. What this amounts to is that each instrument is a part of the overall jigsaw where no piece obscures another piece by playing over it at the same pitch. Listen to the early Tamla Motown records, especially singles by the Supremes, to see how this works. This art is almost dead in an age where a computer can fill every millisecond with sound, whether required or not. This is an extension of the argument that says listeners must never hear any silence in their lives. Musical notation allows symbols for notes *and* silences, making a silence, however short, a bona fide part of music. Some bands understand this – others don't. Silence can be a potent force in music and those that use it well have an advantage over the rest. One of the masters of the pregnant pause is the Rolling Stones' Keith Richards whose stop start riffs add so much to the power of the Stones' music.

Germany's interpretation of the rock 'n' roll blueprint has always been one of the more interesting. Kraftwerk, for example, appeared to have filed it in the bin and then proceeded to invent their own blueprint, just for the hell of it. In fact their ideas were so advanced that the instruments didn't exist that could play their music, so they set about inventing and then constructing them to order. In retrospect, they were miles ahead of their time in bringing electronic music to the masses, even if some of their stuff was a bit too robotic to stomach.

However, my all time favourite slice of electronic music is not German, but British and it was created by Ron Grainer and Delia Derbyshire in the BBC Radiophonic Workshop. In case you haven't guessed, it is the original Dr Who theme and it is as stunning now as it was then. To think that this was made in 1963 without the aid of synthesisers, samplers or computers makes it all the more special. The awareness that each 'voice' was created by electronic test equipment or manually created effects and pieced together, one note at a time, onto tape and then finally merged onto a single master tape ensures its place as supreme creativity. Remember also that this music was a product of pure creation, not performance and you begin to understand its singular quality. With its hypnotic riff and ringing melody, it predates Kraftwerk by some ten plus years yet it still sounds strange and forceful and is more than a match for 'Autobahn' or 'Trans Euro Express'. There are still one or two items that British citizens can be proud of and this is undoubtedly one of them.

German bands from Faust to Tangerine Dream and Can have always been a bit outside the mainstream and have been no less successful for it. In the 1980s I followed a German band called Propaganda for a time. They were signed up by Paul Morley for his ZTT label (which was also home to Frankie Goes to Hollywood) and comprised a bonkers line-up of two female vocalists, one of whom sang and the other only spoke or shouted, a drummer/percussionist (ex-Dusseldorf Symphony Orchestra, no less) and a keyboard player. The remainder of the band was composed of session musicians brought in especially for either studio or live work. The industrial strength rhythm section and peculiar interplay between the two vocalists was one of rock's more intriguing creations. Their debut album 'A Secret Wish' would still grace my all time favourites list even though Trevor Horn's classic 1980s production now sounds a little dated. The rhythms are compulsive, the melodies assured and Claudia Brücken's Germanic singing voice glides effortlessly over the general cacophony with consummate ease. I have a video recording of them playing live on the infamous 1980s TV programme, The Tube and they were magnificently dotty. In it they do a storming version of 'P Machinery' that welds an irrepressible dance beat to the sort of Teutonic melody that Beethoven might have added to one of his symphonies when he was feeling in a particularly good mood. They then follow this with a two-part version of 'Duel' that appears to represent heaven and hell. The first section is treated as a percussive hell on earth with Susanne Freytag yelling the lyrics over a clatter of rhythms and the second a softer, more reflective part with Brücken's nasal voice a welcome heavenly relief. In fact, on reflection Claudia Brücken was a sadly underrated singer in a rather offbeat way. Clearly, label owner Morley believed so as he eventually married her.

I have never really been a fan of French rock for the reason that they tend to stick to their own language and I just can't get past the images of Johnny Hallyday and Charles Aznavour. But when the music is instrumental there are some worthwhile avenues to explore. Jean-Michel Jarre springs to mind as an obvious candidate and some of his earlier less showy work was well worth a listen. More recently, Air has favoured us with their superb 'Moon Safari' album. Both these artists tend towards the spacey atmospheric style of instrumental which perhaps represents the laid back character of the French.

Similarly, other than PFM in the 1970s, no Italian rock band has registered on my radar and accordingly I am hideously under-represented in output from two of Europe's largest countries.

Although it may be stretching the definition of Europe to include Iceland, there is definitely something strange at work in the musings of Björk Gudmundsdóttir. There is no doubt that Björk is one of the true innovators working in music today and there is also no doubt that she has been able to follow her own leanings without the aid of the rock 'n' roll blueprint which would have hampered her creativity to the point of destruction. The true source of her individuality has begun to reveal itself with each progressive album and it is Icelandic folk music. She has admitted as much by employing the services of the Icelandic Octet, a group of string players who specialise in Icelandic music, on her 'Homogenic' album. Her fusion of rock and folk is certainly one of the most boundary redefining forces to have emerged from a non-UK European country and in many ways shows the rest of us the way forward.

In the final analysis, Eurorock is something that should be sampled but only with extreme caution. It is no surprise that only 5% of my entire music collection is attributable to European and new world artists. The remainder hail from the traditional and dependable UK and North America.

Beyond the confines of Europe, on the opposite side of the globe in Australia there also exists a native folk input which when added to the rock blueprint provides another shade to the overall colour scheme. Men At Work, Savage Garden and INXS all have that vague antipodean variety that separates them from the more orthodox Western bands, and it was probably the Seekers who started the trend of pushing native folk music into the mainstream in the 1960s. Of particular merit were a band called Frente who produced a couple of albums in the 1990s. Comprising a standard three-piece band fronted by singer Angie Hart, they successfully crossed rock sensibilities with Australian folk music and ended up sounding how you might expect modern skiffle to turn out if electronic instruments were used rather than old tea chests and your mum's washboard. Interestingly, Angie Hart turned up again recently singing at the fictional nightspot 'The Bronze' in the TV programme 'Buffy the Vampire Slayer'. Buffy fans were always treated to a wide variety of artists performing at this legendary venue whose roster included Sean Lennon and Aimee Mann as Joss Whedon, its producer, is a self-proclaimed music fan. Angie also sings the haunting song 'Blue', written by her together with Whedon, that threads its way through the edgy episode 'Conversations with Dead People' in the programme's final season.

So, in conclusion, music is a bit like wine. It can be sweet and intoxicating or bitter and disappointing, but the best thing is it can be made all over the world given the right environment. Wine-making involves, I believe, growing grapes and then extracting the juice and bottling it, but despite the uniformity of manufacture, all wines taste different partly because the soil in a given location lends its flavour to the grapes and therefore to the resultant wine. So it is with music. The rock 'n' roll blueprint remains basically the same worldwide, but the local musical traditions always seem to find their way in to the final flavour. As with wine this is a good thing as it continually produces new variations on old methods and every once in a while a rare vintage will surface. It is also evident that local markets are aware of these variations and cater for them.

In America, which traditionally had a predominantly European based population, there are now increasing proportions of Hispanic and South American peoples. Consequently, no American artist worth his or her salt works through an entire career without releasing at least one single with a Latin beat. Madonna did it with 'La Isla Bonita' and Britney Spears has done it with 'Born to Make You Happy' and I'm sure there are others.

The music business is rife with variety and knowing your global markets is part of financial success, but it is still worth uncovering those little known blends, something that the late John Peel did with unnerving consistency. He will be sorely missed.

Chapter Eight

ROLL OVER BEETHOVEN

There are many things in life that, for one reason or another, you end up having to do without the least desire to do them. There's mowing the lawn or decorating the spare room or any amount of things to do with your working life and generally the only feeling experienced on their completion is relief. This progression from foreboding to relief would certainly apply to my musical career at secondary school were it not for one thing and that is that subsequently, the relief slowly transformed into a grudging gratitude that I was pushed into expanding my boundaries.

Take the school choir, for example. My school maintained both an orchestra and a full four-part choir, much to the credit of the music department, and every year all new intake were auditioned for a place in the choir. Now, as a newcomer, I was as disinterested as the next boy in joining up for this type of extra-curricular but, as a naïve twelve year old, I didn't understand that if you sang deliberately badly at the audition, as did most of my more worldly peers, you wouldn't be picked, so suddenly there I was, a new recruit to the intricacies of classical harmony singing. At first I hated it for interrupting good football time with endless rehearsals, but little by little and against my better judgement, I started to enjoy it. I think it was the annual Christmas carol concert that started it and when we were taught the harmony lines to favourites like 'Hark! The Herald Angels Sing' and 'O Come all Ye Faithful' it became fun to sing in a manner that made your head swim with a sort of euphoria. Moreover, it was even more fun to sing these parts at gatherings outside of the school environment. Much later, when I graduated to

University, I met others who knew how to sing harmony and we would go around the University carol services and sit in the congregation as a sort of clandestine barbershop quartet only without the striped shirts, subversively singing the harmony lines when supposedly carrying the melody. It's the kind of knowledge that you don't easily forget and I still do it now at church carol services, much to the annoyance of family and friends.

But it was Mozart that permanently instilled a love of choral singing in my being and the work that enthralled me was his Requiem Mass in D minor. The school choir plus orchestra had undertaken to perform parts of this work for an end of year concert and it was the combination of the story behind the work and the work itself that finally breached my defences. For those of you that have not seen the film 'Amadeus', the background, briefly, is as follows. In July 1791 Mozart receives a visit from a mysterious stranger who has come to deliver a commission for a Requiem Mass on behalf of an unnamed principal (subsequently thought to be Count von Walsegg). An advance is paid and more money promised on provision that the work be completed within one month. Time, however, drifts by and at the end of the month, the piece has yet to be started, let alone completed, and Mozart has then to leave for Prague for a premiere of another of his works. On his return, exhausted and enfeebled, he starts work on his commission but soon realises that his health is failing badly and indeed, he dies in December 1791 of broncho-pneumonia leaving the Requiem uncompleted. His wife, eager to collect the fee, turns to Mozart's pupil, Sussmayr, to complete the work in order that it be presented ostensibly as written by Mozart and this he does. Poor old Sussmayr has come in for a lot of criticism from music lovers over the years but I think he did a great job in developing the various parts from Mozart's scribbled notes, some of which only amounted to the first eight bars.

To my impressionable mind, the vision of the dying composer, staring into the void of approaching death, yet forced to write a Requiem Mass for someone else knowing it was ultimately his own, was tremendously powerful. The story translates directly to the music and it vividly reflects Mozart's state of mind. The whole piece has a desperation and urgency about it that is quite gripping and its baroque style is ideally suited to the horror of death. Since that time I have loved choral work in all its forms from religious church choirs to Brian Wilson's inventive arrangements for the Beach Boys immaculate harmonies. There is nothing quite like the human voice when blended with others to create a sense of awe and I have felt it often when listening to choral music. In particular, there is something uplifting about religious pieces performed in churches, with their echoing acoustics that always says more to me about the achievement of man than the achievement of God, the subject the music is designed to promote.

By this time in my schooling, it was getting uncomfortably near the point of no return as far as choosing 'O' level subjects was concerned. The system then in force was that there was a series of five no-choice subjects such as English and Maths, and then a pool of remaining subjects where each individual could make a choice of three others. Having garnered a taste of musical harmony, I decided it was worth having a shot at music 'O' level. The decision to be made was not unlike grasping the proverbial double-edged sword as the course was divided into some areas in which I was really interested and others that I wouldn't normally give exercise book room. The problem being that the one was inextricably linked to the other. I discovered that there were three sections: lives of famous composers, four study works and musical theory. Theory was the bit that really interested me, and analysing classical works, I gauged, might be OK, but there again, might not but composers I could really do without. After a fair amount of shall I or shan't I, I finally opted to ditch it and do something else, but then again I really wanted to know a bit about musical theory and although I'd read hundreds of interviews with iconic rock stars who would swear blind that they knew nothing about reading or writing music, there was something nagging at me which said, 'they might be genius but you're not and you're going to need all the help you can get'. I signed up the next day.

After two years' study, I still knew next to nothing about the lives of classical composers but the theory was fascinating. It included learning to write for voices and constructing four-part harmony – exactly the stuff I'd been singing in the choir – melody writing, chord construction and all sorts of useful knowledge that could just as easily be utilised in a popular context. Even the set works weren't bad. Unfortunately, the main study work was Beethoven's first symphony, which I found tedious, insipid and ultimately boring. Even with the experience of time on my side, I cannot learn to love it and I am still mostly disinterested in symphonic works. The second was Stravinsky's ballet, the 'Rite of Spring'. This was much more to my taste and it remains my favourite classical piece to this day. Quite what the premiere audience made of it in 1913, I find difficult to imagine, but the fact that there were riots recorded suggests a clue to the reactions provoked. No matter, it is a passionately primal work of pulsing, complex rhythms and aching discords which appealed to me in a way that standard classical fare did not. Stravinsky clearly decided to throw away the rule book when it came to writing this piece, yet it also has an undertone of Russian melancholy in its melodies that cries out to the listener when set against the violent dynamics and rule breaking harmony.

The third piece was J S Bach's Italian Concerto for harpsichord and was my second favourite of the four. This solo piece in three movements taught me the merits of key modulation as a method of introducing interest, surprise and excitement to music and the use of the semitone in melody writing to imply such modulation. In Bach's day, the solo instrument was the harpsichord but its major drawback was that it had no natural dynamic, that is, the same volume of sound would result however hard a key was pressed, so it was no good just trying to play louder or softer to create drama. What was needed was *musical* drama, not dynamic drama and the use of trills (rapid alternating between two notes) and in particular, key modulation were two of the tools used to create it. For example, a melody in the key of C major will use the notes C,D,E,F,G,A and B, but by moving the melody to the semitone between say, D and E, E flat, a note that does not belong to the C major scale, the key of either C minor, E flat major or A flat major is implied. This produces a surprise, as we are not 'expecting' a note outside of the established scale, nor the harmony that comes with it.

The recording we used at school was actually a piano transcription so it was a revelation when I found a true recording recently featuring a reconditioned harpsichord, originally made in Paris in 1751. Without the natural dynamics of a piano the piece shows more clearly how Bach was able to simulate musical light and shade by use of the notes only. It is truly masterful.

The last piece was Rossini's 'William Tell Overture', which if you can listen to this and not picture the Lone Ranger riding through arid desert landscapes on a white horse, you must be either very young or a Trappist monk.

All these classical composers have influenced the way I look at popular music and it is no surprise that my favourite artists today use Bach's semitonal melodies to imply key modulations, Mozart's choral harmony and Stravinsky's edgy instrumentation and primal rhythms.

Having passed music at 'O' Level I decided that 'A' Level would be a bridge too far as it involved learning to play an orchestral instrument to a absurd level of competence and all manner of off-putting ventures. Anyway, I had bigger fish to fry and scurried on to commence part two of my master plan: learning to play the guitar. This initially posed a bit of a problem as I didn't own one, but fate came to my rescue in the form of a week's work, during the holidays, helping a friend of my father's run his one man band landscape gardening business.

I had noted diligently that all rock stars started out on the road to success by doing highly unrelated jobs and I decided mine would be landscape gardening. However, what I hadn't bargained for was that it was backbreakingly hard work and involved a lot of digging, moving earth and materials around in a wheelbarrow, weeding, mowing and other strenuous activities. The week's itinerary would follow the same pattern. The van would arrive outside my house at eight o'clock every morning and the two of us would rattle away to yet another wilderness in the suburbs that required our attention. Lunch would be eaten at about noon, usually whilst sitting in the van to shelter from the torrential rain and after thirty minutes or so, off we'd go again. By the end of the week, I could hardly move a muscle and vowed that manual labour must be avoided at all costs, thus motivating me vigorously for my sixth form studies. Nevertheless, my effort paid me £15 for the week (equivalent to about £125 at the time of writing) and this was just enough to secure that steel strung, three-quarter size Eko acoustic guitar that I had seen hanging up in the local music shop.

Ever since that enlightening moment with Terry Kath's guitar solo, I had fancied having a go at learning the guitar, but until now I hadn't really been within striking distance of owning one. Although my parents hadn't seemingly passed on any instrument playing genes, I took comfort from the fact that my sister had managed to learn the recorder at primary school, so there must be some propensity to play somewhere in the family. I'd also been press-ganged into learning the bassoon at school but hadn't really got to grips with it and had given it up at the first opportunity. After all, the only rock tracks I could think of that used a bassoon were 'Cheap Day Return' from Jethro Tull's 'Aqualung' album and 'Down to You' from Joni Mitchell's 'Court and Spark' so it wasn't exactly the instrument of choice for most rock musicians. Now that the chance had come to do something I felt was more relevant, I had to grasp it lest it slip away. Whilst all this was whirling in my brain, I couldn't help but wonder whether Jimmy Page had been worried by all this trivia when he got started. I suspected not.

The following Saturday found me entering the St Albans Music Centre on Holywell Hill (just down from the outdoor activities shop – sign outside: 'Now is the season of our discount tents') clutching my £15 and trying to steady my wildly beating heart. The shop seemed to have been in this location for as long as anyone could remember (and still exists today), but in the early 1970s it was in a bit of a crisis of confidence, having for many years been the orchestral musical instrument and sheet music supplier to the classically inclined, it was now having to cater for the budding rock star and so provided a choice of about half a dozen guitars and a handful of popular music song books, tucked away at the back of its tiny sales area, amongst the violins and flutes. The reason for my apprehension was the thought of having to buy an instrument that I knew nothing about and worse still, couldn't play a note on. What if I was asked if I wanted to try it – in front of people? I didn't even know the riff to 'Smoke on the Water'. What I really wanted to say was; 'I'd like to buy that one, please, because it looks nice', but somehow this didn't seem the right approach to an assistant who was used to people coming in to buy French horns and whatnot and dashing off a few bars of Mozart's Horn Concerto in E flat just to get a feel of the thing. So after a furtive ten minutes or so spent eyeing up the merchandise, I screwed up enough courage to come clean and inform the assistant that I was an absolute beginner, but would like to buy a guitar and would that one on the wall be appropriate. Luckily, or unsurprisingly, dependent upon how cynical you are, he said it was and the deal was done with the minimum of fuss. I had also spotted a small booklet entitled 'The Paul Simon Songbook' which contained the music to 60s anthems such as 'The Sound of Silence' and 'I Am a Rock' and others I recognised, so an additional 40p went into adding this to my purchases and happily, I set off for home.

So far, so good, but now I had two further difficulties to surmount. The first was that my new Paul Simon songbook only showed the melody line with the guitar chords, such as C, G and Am, written over the top. There were no diagrams to show the fingering necessary to play each chord. This might have been a categorical disaster were it not for my recently obtained musical knowledge which was to come to my aid by allowing me to work out the notes required in each chord and thus discover the fingering patterns. The second difficulty was not so easily fixed and that was actually trying to play the instrument in a manner that sounded even vaguely musical. All of a sudden my fingers would stop obeying me and would flail hopelessly about trying to form the correct patterns. Chord changes took about five minutes each whilst I fought with the errant fingers and all the while a feeling of disappointment was gathering. I laboured on for days trying to learn the song 'April She Will Come' which will be known to anyone who has seen the film 'The Graduate', as it only has four chords in it and the necessity for change was not too frequent, but even so, the experience was not how I had imagined it would be. The steel strings bit into my soft fingertips like hot knives and the chord shapes just would not form quickly enough to effect a swift seamless change. I think it was about this point that the vision of a lucrative career as a rock star began to fade.

But like all learning undertakings, practice paid off in the longer term and I was determined to succeed having shelled out my entire week's wages, gained through sweat and blood, for this opportunity. Eventually, after a few weeks of hard labour, my fingers began to harden and the chord patterns began to become second nature. I bought more sheet music and learned more chords, which I was able to assimilate with confidence. It was only then that I realised, with some exultation, that I was, in my own small way, a musician.

Being an amateur musician is like joining a club where you don't know any of the other members. Initially, it is a lonely existence, but then slowly other musicians reveal themselves by dropped references or actions every now and then throughout the rest of your life. It is a shared passion, but at the same time, generally a very low-key attribute that may never become apparent in people you know. It can surprise you when someone you have known for ages suddenly sits down at the piano and plays a flawless rendition of Beethoven's 'Moonlight Sonata', as once happened to me. But most of all, playing a musical instrument is a wonderfully recreational pastime, it can soothe and exhilarate, dependent on mood, and always bestows a special feeling of creativity on the player. I'm glad I made the effort all those years ago even if it didn't lead to fame and riches.

Being a guitarist of sorts, I have a certain bias towards the instrument, but if there is one other member of the musical fraternity that I really cannot abide, it is the saxophone. Once upon a time, I didn't really mind it. Chicago had a sax player and it didn't bother me, but then came the day of reckoning that was to change everything. I think it was probably 'Baker Street' by Gerry Rafferty that initiated this loathing and that infernal sax riff. If there is one thing guaranteed to accelerate an initial indifference into full-blown loathing, it is finding that everyone you meet just *loves* that saxophone riff. The knife twister is that those same people have no recollection of the sublime guitar solo nestling at the end of the song, just when you think it's about to end. At this point Rafferty's guitar produces an uplifting moment of alternating sustained notes and runs, which outshines the sax easily, yet nobody goes on and on about that solo, do they?

After 'Baker Street', I could no longer listen to any sax work and my loathing reached psychopathic proportions. So it was all the more amusing when the following scenario played out on the TV quiz show, Family Fortunes – the one where contestants have to guess the audience's most popular replies to given questions. In this instance, the question was:

Name a brass musical instrument. The contestant confidently rattled through the components of a brass band such as trumpet, trombone, cornet and tuba, which were all correct but had failed to reveal the most popular answer. With time running out, the poor contestant racked his brain trying to think of obscure brass instruments like the euphonium and the flugelhorn, but to no avail. His time ran out and the answer that the majority of the audience had given was then revealed as, yes you've guessed it; the saxophone. The contestant looked dumbfounded and with good reason, the saxophone is not a brass instrument at all, but a woodwind instrument by virtue of its sound being generated by blowing across a reed in the same manner as a clarinet. The fact that it has a metal body is irrelevant. Obviously, the studio manager didn't know this either as the result was allowed to stand and the contestant trudged back to his family despondently.

Since then, I have tried to ignore the saxophone in rock music in the hope that it will go away, but the signs aren't good and if anybody else tells me that the sax riff in 'Baker Street' is simply wonderful, I shall not be responsible for my actions.

Chapter Nine

THE WORST BAND IN THE WORLD

Even though I have been collecting music all my life, there are times when a stab of apprehension grips me like an icy chill and I think that I will never find another band or artist that I will like. It takes the form of a hideous dread that this is the end of the road and I will fritter away my last days browsing through the Easy Listening sections looking for that rare Andy Williams album. Yet, almost invariably this proves to be incorrect, apart from the Andy Williams bit, but nevertheless, for a lingeringly anxious period the fear is real that when my favourite bands split or cease recording, it is the end of the long affair.

In true Mr Micawber style, something always turns up and this set me thinking about why it does, and what it is that attracts me to certain bands or artists in the first place. Could it be fashion, or lack of it, or the band's name or the fact that I liked their last single or the album cover or what? In fact, I did once buy an album by the look of the cover alone. It was '77' by Talking Heads, a band I'd never heard of at the time, but that bright red cover was too good to pass over. Luckily, it turned out to be crackingly good, but I never tried it again. Having considered all the albums in my possession the answer seems to be that it's because I've no taste at all and like to humour the weirder members of society and unfortunately there is evidence for this assertion. At the end of the 1980s the BBC put together a splendid three-hour TV programme summarising the pop music of the decade and to give the programme some structure, divided it into sections. What rather alarmed me was that most of my favourite bands and artists appeared in the section named 'Barking Mad'.

There they were, Julian Cope fronting the Teardrop Explodes looking completely insane in a leather flying jacket, Cyndi Lauper giving another over the top life or death performance, Bauhaus, Dexy's Midnight Runners, all of them one bar short of a chorus. But, and this is the point, anyone who looks and thinks the way we all do is not going to come up with anything different from the rest of us. What makes these people so interesting is the very fact that they are different, or mad if you like and create art that would not occur to most of us. Although I will admit to liking these types of artists, I don't think this is the sole reason that attracts me to certain bands. The other major theme I can discern is connected with songwriting so, in order to preserve some dignity; I'm going with that.

Songwriting and songwriters are subjects that have fascinated me since I could first read record labels for myself. The first thing I would do on purchasing a new recording would be to see who wrote what and memorise it, for let's face it, no band can survive without a decent song, irrespective of style or image unless you're Sique Sique Sputnik, but a decent song can survive without a band. Songs are the lifeblood of popular music yet the people who have the creativity to write them well are few and far between. A good wheeze is to ask people whether they know who Diane Warren is. Most people have no idea and not surprisingly as she is not an artist in her own right, yet they have probably spent the last 20 years or so of their lives listening to songs she has written. The diverse list of artists who have covered her songs includes Elton John, Tina Turner, Barbra Streisand, Aretha Franklin, Roy Orbison, 'N Sync, Gloria Estefan, Britney Spears, Christina Aguilera, Whitney Houston, Enrique Iglesias, Aerosmith, Celine Dion, Mary J. Blige and LeAnn Rimes. One of her most recent hits was 'Too Lost in You' performed by the Sugababes, a wonderfully emotional song by someone who knows how to write and it shows. It just proves how unknown and undervalued these people are in terms of public recognition but I don't suppose they go short of a few bob so perhaps I'm overreacting. The trouble is I've always wanted to be one.

Lone performing songwriters are easy to spot as they advertise as themselves and the listener either likes what they hear or not, as the case may be. There are no grey areas here, what you hear is what you get. Just for the record, my own favourites include well-known artists such as Elton John, Joni Mitchell, Kate Bush, Tori Amos and Suzanne Vega and perhaps less well-known artists like Juliana Hatfield, P.J. Harvey, Julian Cope and the criminally underrated Aimee Mann. All these people have one thing in common and that is that they turn out great tunes, great lyrics or both and for that they have my undying admiration because it's not that easy. Believe me, I've tried.

Bands, however, are more interesting in that they have a collective name which shields the writers from public gaze and prevents the casual listener from knowing who, in the band, is responsible, if anybody, for writing the material. Bands also have an internal dynamic when it comes to putting together a few tunes for the next release and the interaction between the members can have a marked effect on the outcome. In my experience, bands can be categorised into the following songwriting groups:

A. Those dominated by a single songwriter.
B. Those that contain a songwriting partnership.
C. Those where everyone has a go.
D. Those that have two dynamically opposed writers.

Naturally, there are those bands that do not write at all but either cover others' material or have songs written specifically for them, but I have excluded them for the purpose of this analysis.

The first group, those that are dominated by a single songwriter, are represented by the following typical examples: Dire Straits (Mark Knopfler), Kinks (Ray Davies), Oasis (Noel Gallagher), Beach Boys (Brian Wilson) and The Who (Pete Townshend). These bands tend to have a life equal to the songwriter's ability to produce good songs and hence only the very best survive for any length of time, verified by the quality of the list above. Unfortunately, unless the remainder of the band have real personality, they will be relegated to the status of backing band and members may change without any discernible difference to the band's sound. The advantage of this set-up is that the writer has absolute control and may be assured that the results are exactly as planned. The downside being that there is no one to criticise when the product is substandard and no one to prick self-indulgence. Also, there tends to be a sameness of style which doesn't always hold your interest unless it is something special. In short, only the best examples are worth a listen.

The second group, those that contain a songwriting partnership, are represented by examples such as: The Smiths (Morrissey/Marr), The Rolling Stones (Jagger/Richards), Abba (Ulvaeus/Andersson) and Led Zeppelin (Plant/Page). In this group, the writing partnerships tend to be functionally split between tunesmith and lyric writer. Because one cannot perform without the other, these partnerships often endure unless, as in the case of the Smiths, personal rather than musical differences threaten. The partnership seems to be one of the most common configurations in rock from Burt Bacharach/Hal David through Elton John/Bernie Taupin to Robbie Williams/Guy Chambers and has the advantage of potentially welding a first class tune to a worthwhile lyric in more cases than most. There are few single songwriters who can manage this consistently although certainly, Joni Mitchell and Elvis Costello may be considered to have managed it and Bob Dylan certainly did. Where there are two people involved there always exists the potential for one to inspire the other hence the problems of the single writer are often circumvented. I can't think of any other reason why the Rolling Stones should still be churning out new material forty years down the line.

The third group, those where everyone has a go at writing may be divided into two sub-groups: those where each writer is individually credited with their own songs and those where the band as a whole is credited. The former group is represented by examples such as Queen and 10cc and the latter by the likes of Yes, Genesis, REM and Radiohead. In this configuration, there is often a confusion of styles unless the band can put their collective stamp on all the material equally. In the former category, interesting results can be obtained by mixing up the writing partnerships in the manner of early 10cc when Stewart, Gouldman, Godley and Creme wrote in various combinations when penning the classic 'Sheet Music' album. In the 'collective' style, the listener has no idea who was responsible as all writing credits are masked under a single band credit. Quite how the writing works is open to debate, but certainly, Genesis have stated that most of their material evolves from jam sessions, so it seems likely that others such as New Order, Siouxsie and the Banshees and Deep Purple who all use the collective credit also function this way. There are many bands that operate as a collective that I like a lot, so there doesn't seem to be anything intrinsically wrong, it's just that I like to know whodunit and this lot have the last page torn out.

But it is the final group, those that have two opposed writers, that is undoubtedly the most interesting of the bunch and it is the group I prefer, as evidenced by the inclusion of most of my favourite bands from mega-stars to not so mega stars – Pink Floyd, XTC, Argent, Curved Air and Fanny. I have always been fascinated by this construction and have dubbed these bands 'Twin Towers' bands as they are dominated by two strong but radically different songwriters. It is always contended that great art comes from pain and in this arrangement there exists a high degree of internal friction, competition and even animosity between the writers, which at first creates a heightened degree of output quality, but unfortunately eventually leads to disaster and an inevitable split. Most of the bands in this category do not survive the turmoil that their arrangement creates and the writers' individual interests tear the partnership asunder. The life cycle of a typical crash and burn Twin Towers band is something like this:

1. Early days. Early songs have a strong 'band' sound but are a cut above their peers. This is a result of the two protagonists working together towards a common goal and putting differences aside. With the help of the rest of the band, each song is arranged in a collective style that makes it immediately recognisable as a band song but gives little clue as to the original writer.

2. Middle period. This is the golden age where the songs produced are generally acknowledged to be the cream of the crop. Each writer is becoming more competent, more competitive and more assured. Two different styles are beginning to emerge as each writer takes control of the arrangement and production of their own material. In this period, the whole is considerably greater than the sum of its parts as each inspires the other and contributes their own ideas to the other's efforts. The range of material is also quite broad as it encompasses the palette of both writers.

3. Final Period. The two writers' styles are diverging significantly and because the band no longer has any say in the arrangements, a band album sounds to the listener like two solo albums, spliced together, with no overall coherence. The writers are beginning to feel constrained within the band format and, eventually, one writer will leave under a cloud of recriminations citing the inevitable 'musical differences'. The band then either folds or continues in a type A 'those dominated by a single writer' configuration.

As you may have already guessed, the ultimate Twin Towers band was the Beatles. Despite the noteworthy contributions of George Harrison, the band was dominated by the Lennon and McCartney song-writing machine. Lennon was perhaps the more instinctive writer, relying on his own sense of rhythm and feel for what sounded good, rather than using strict musical conventions. Whilst his melodies were often simple and intuitive, his songs would often contain odd numbers of bars or strange rhythmic anomalies that gave them a unique quality. McCartney, by contrast, took a more studious approach and relied on his talent for melody and musical construction. That is not to say he was strictly conventional, the ideas to use tape loops and other studio tricks were often his. But it is the mechanism whereby each writer adds ideas to and criticises the work of the other, even when one writer is working alone, that creates the Twin Towers effect and when this was operating at its peak, it took the Beatles to a higher plain and to worldwide acclaim. The band's career trajectory was almost identical to that outlined above, from the early collaborative days to the middle period heights of Lennon's 'Strawberry Fields' (unconventional rhythmic flow) and McCartney's 'Penny Lane' (perfect melody) to the final diversion of styles and eventual split.

The Pink Floyd is another classic Twin Towers Band. Following Syd Barrett's departure and the subsequent hiring of Dave Gilmour, the standard configuration was complete. With assistance from Rick Wright, the Twin Towers of Roger Waters and Dave Gilmour took the band from their psychedelic beginnings through the monster 'Dark Side of the Moon' to their inevitable split when Waters left the band. The ingredients at work here were Water's ear for a measured, stately rhythm and a dark, gloomy introspective lyric and by contrast, Gilmour's sunny extrovert outlook and lightness of touch. In the final stages of the band's career arc, when the opposing styles of the two writers were becoming quite distinct, they produced the monumentally grandiose double album, 'The Wall'. At this stage, by all accounts, Waters and Gilmour were barely on speaking terms. One of the better-known tracks from this piece of Waters paranoia is 'Comfortably Numb', a song of increasing isolation within the rock world they themselves inhabited and it is this song that shows the strength of the Twin Towers band, even in adversity.

The song is constructed conventionally comprising a verse followed by chorus. The verse is typically a Waters product consisting of a broody, rather sinister lyric over a moderate, measured beat. The feeling is very claustrophobic and gloomy until the chorus arrives courtesy of Gilmour. This section of the song suddenly blossoms as if all the curtains in a dark room have been flung aside and the sun has entered. The melody rises up almost joyously even though the lyric is wistful, rather than joyful, before returning to the murky enclosed verse. In the middle of the song is a rather perfunctory guitar solo from Gilmour that rather drags and lacks interest, but at the end of the song something rather wonderful happens. As the band gears up for the Coda, Gilmour switches his guitar tone to a much grittier, echoey sound and unleashes one of his finest solos, full of yearning blues runs and string bends that tears at your soul whilst all the while Water's ponderous rhythm, as tight as a vice, continues its stately way to the fade. This is one of the few moments of recorded music that I genuinely do not wish to end and when the fade out approaches I am desperate for more. The whole piece is a consummate marriage of the writers' two opposing styles even to the point where, at the dénouement, they act against one another; yet still manage to produce a thrilling piece of music.

Probably the most typical Twin Towers band in my collection is Argent, which attempted to join together the forces of Rod Argent and Russ Ballard. Rod had just dissolved the Zombies (another Twin Towers band comprising songwriters Argent and Chris White) and was looking to set up his own outfit. Rod's style is studious verging on the classical with a bent towards jazz, so it seemed a trifle strange that he should team up with Russ Ballard, a down to earth rock 'n' roller, much beloved of the three-chord trick and raucous vocal. Two completely different approaches, one could not imagine, but for a time it worked spectacularly. After the usual early period of pussy footing around each other's proclivities, the golden period started around 1971 with 'Hold your Head Up'. This is actually an Argent/White composition, given away by its precise harmony and use of key, but with Ballard's rock vocals and strident guitar in the mix, the piece seems to be lifted to another level. This, in my opinion, is where the potential of a good Twin Towers band reaches fruition and in the action of mixing two disparate styles produces a hybrid that is better than either. True to style, Ballard eventually cracked under the strain of not enough rock 'n' roll in amongst the classical jazz and left. Argent disbanded a few distinctly non-rock albums later.

The same story bedevilled Fanny where June Millington's Californian folk inspired roots were put into confrontation with Nickey Barclay's bluesy funk which, whilst initially producing an interesting outcome, led to Millington's departure and the collapse of the band. Curved Air, as I have already mentioned, pitted the haunting violin melodies of Daryl Way up against the electronic experimentation of Francis Monkman with unique results until both walked out in a huff. Way eventually returned but it was never the same.

Twin Towers writing partnerships are not always to be found in the big successful bands but will turn up anywhere. The Go-Gos, for example. This all female band, fronted by Belinda Carlisle and formed in the wake of the new wave, contained the guitarist/writers; Charlotte Caffey and Jane Weidlin and they enjoyed a fair amount of success with their energetic take on post-punk powerpop. Inevitably, the band split and Jane Weidlin had a brief solo career which produced the infectious hit single 'Rush Hour', whilst Charlotte Caffey contributed songs for Belinda Carlisle's early solo albums and formed a short-lived band called the Graces, with Meredith Brooks and Gia Ciambotti.

The Go-Gos are also interesting because they may have uncovered more information about the life of a Twin Towers band in that, having split, they have followed a recently growing trend and have since reformed. It seems there may be a further phase to the Twin Towers career arc that has not previously revealed itself due to insufficient duration. Perhaps, if the period of the bands' existence is lengthened, we may see a mass reformation of long since splintered Twin Towers bands, assuming all members are alive and willing. There is an inkling of evidence for this twist in the saga by the fact that Pink Floyd have just welcomed back Roger Waters into the fold for the first time in twenty-six years in order for the original band to play at the Live8 2005 concert in Hyde Park. I await further developments with interest, but frankly, the thought of all the bands on my Twin Towers list, now mostly into middle age, churning out their old hits (or not, as the case may be) doesn't fill me with much anticipation.

There is no doubt in my mind that it is the forced mixing of styles that makes Twin Towers bands so special and the fact that the Beatles, arguably the greatest band in history, was built on this foundation only confirms my belief.

But this melting pot approach is not only the hallmark of good Twin Towers bands but of popular music in general. Rock 'n' Roll itself could be argued to be the mixing of black American blues and white American country musics. The Beach Boys' sound was a direct fusion of the doo-wop harmony singers of the 1950s and the rock 'n' roll of Chuck Berry. In many areas the way forward is often the mixing of styles to create a new one and that is why pop music has managed to reinvent itself constantly over a period of many decades. It is also the reason why, when I find that a new band has a promising set-up involving two dominant writers, my ears prick up in anticipation of a new avenue ripe for discovery. And if they have a female singer, so much the better.

Chapter Ten

OLD SONGS, NEW SONGS

One evening, whilst settled down to watch my favourite bit of television fantasy; 'Buffy the Vampire Slayer', something happened which shocked me more than I care to admit. The episode in question was one where the majority of the script is delivered in song as if it were a musical film. To further this connection with the musical format, an Overture plays during the first few minutes to introduce key musical themes, and it was the initial melody that caused me to scratch my head in bewilderment. The tune comprised only a few simple notes and was driven along by lush orchestral strings in the manner of a classic Disney film. The problem was that I had this vague notion that I recognised the tune, but couldn't place it for the life of me. It was not until much, much later, when I had watched the episode several times that it dawned on me what it was. It was the programme's signature tune – something that I had heard countless times over several years and which I know backwards – yet I hadn't recognised it.

Normally, the signature tune is performed by the rock band, Nerf Herder and it thunders along with a clatter of drums and swathes of distorted guitars, but in its delicate orchestral form, I had not recognised it and it is this that shocked me. I realised then that whilst I thought I knew the tune, what I actually knew was the unique performance of the tune and not the tune itself.

In his illuminating book about major musical innovations, 'Big Bangs', composer, writer and broadcaster, Howard Goodall describes this phenomenon at length, but the key point of his argument is that since the invention of recorded music, what we all associate with a song is often the performance by the artist involved and not the tune in isolation. In the days before recorded music, the only method of reproducing a favourite song was to purchase the sheet music and play it for yourself. This conjures up images of Bertie Wooster banging out incompetent versions of the latest show tunes, or families gathered around pianos in dark Victorian parlours, but nevertheless, this is how music was distributed to the public. It is not a coincidence that the method of gauging the popularity of contemporary songs right up until the 1950s was by the sales of sheet music, not recordings. Given these circumstances, where every rendition of a song was almost certainly different, the only common aspect would be the song itself, hence the one thing that everyone would know was the melody and the interpretation was secondary. This probably explains why we are able to recognise a tune like, 'Happy Birthday' instantly, whether it be played by a brass band in the park, an orchestra in a concert hall or simply at home on a kazoo. It is because we have no preconceived idea of its performance. On the other hand, how often do we initially struggle to recognise popular hits such as say, Queen's 'Bohemian Rhapsody' when it is played out of context by the aforementioned brass band or orchestra? What we are expecting to hear is Queen's unique interpretation and when we don't hear it, we are momentarily confused.

And this is why, in this age of unlimited access to recorded music, making a known song your own is more difficult and why a new interpretation of a previously successful popular song always begs comparison with the earlier performance and will fail unless it is significantly better or different.

There is nothing intrinsically wrong with covering others' work but it is apparent that some bands can do cover versions with some invention and others can't for toffee. Of those that can't are, unfortunately, one of my favourite 1960s bands; the Zombies. There is no doubt that their own work is consistently worthy but to hear Colin Blunstone struggling through old rhythm and blues standards like 'I Got My Mojo Working' and 'Sticks and Stones' is enough to make you thankful that modern CD players have a skip button. The only cover that really works for them is their rhythmically reworked version of George Gershwin's 'Summertime', which is more interesting, purely because it is musically more inventive. The other surprise is the Beach Boys whose dreadful interpretation of 'California Dreamin'' takes a very small edge off their largely unblemished canon.

I have four favourite covers artists and these are: Siouxsie and the Banshees, The Bangles, Manfred Mann and Tori Amos. The first three have had as much success with their covers of others' material as with their own and it is because they have a talent to make songs their own that this situation exists. Siouxsie's trio of hits, The Beatles' 'Dear Prudence', Bob Dylan's 'Wheels on Fire' and Iggy Pop's 'The Passenger' are lessons in how to reinvent songs in your own image so as to divert attention from the original version. The Bangles are also adept at this as evidenced by their covers of Princes' 'Manic Monday', Simon and Garfunkel's 'Hazy Shade of Winter' and Katrina and the Waves' 'Going Down to Liverpool'. Manfred Mann, in his later reincarnation as the Earth Band owes Bruce Springsteen a few beers for the success they have eked out of covering his 'Blinded by the Light' and 'Spirits in the Night'. Mann obviously obtained the taste for doing cover versions of others' songs after early success with Bob Dylan's 'Mighty Quinn'. All of these reinterpretations succeed because they create an interest in their own right and do not invite the listener to compare them unfavourably with previous versions. A good test of a successful cover is often to listen to the original version and find it disappointing.

Often, it is the more bizarre reinterpretations that are remembered, such as Rolf Harris's unforgettable rendition of Led Zeppelin's 'Stairway to Heaven', accompanied by those stalwarts of the rock musician's armoury, the wobbleboard and the didgeridoo, but most people would probably pick

Jimi Hendrix's version of Dylan's 'All Along the Watchtower' as the archetypal cover. In fact, Dylan reverted to performing this version in preference to his own – surely the biggest compliment.

A major reinterpreter of well-known songs is Tori Amos, as anyone who has heard her bleak piano and voice renditions of Curt Cobain's 'Smells Like Teen Spirit' and the Rolling Stones' 'Angie' will attest. She has the knack of making sufficient subtle changes to allow a slightly different perspective of the song to emerge. In particular, she has the ability to rephrase the lyrics of the song, without actually changing the words, so that a new meaning is hinted at. To achieve this effect, the singer needs to consciously adjust their intonation and phrasing, as it is all too easy to follow the previous artist's vocal style, as anyone who has sung karaoke versions of well-known hits will recognise. This seems to have been the case where the Corrs' version of Fleetwood Mac's, 'Dreams' is concerned. Andrea Corr slips neatly into Stevie Nicks' original phrasing with such ease that it is difficult to tell the difference.

One of the best covers I know is a version of Lesley Gore's 1963 hit, 'It's My Party' by Dave Stewart (not the Eurythmics' David A Stewart) and Barbara Gaskin. Chalk and cheese immediately spring to mind when considering the musical credentials of this duo but it didn't seem to stop them forming a highly productive collaboration. Dave Stewart was the long haired keyboard player of the deeply progressive 1970s band, Hatfield and the North and Barbara Gaskin, a member of the Canterbury folk ensemble, Spirogyra, but together they concocted one of the most intriguing and downright quirky cover versions of all time. Lesley Gore's original was very much in the style of its time and hitched a teenage melodrama so beloved of peer groups like the Shangri-Las to a moderately bouncy, 1950s rhythm. Gore's vocal performance is suitably tragic, befitting her juvenile persona, as the story of her birthday party turns sour. Stewart and Gaskin's version, however, is much darker revealing a more resigned and almost sinister content to the story. The chorus is taken, if anything at a slightly faster pace and gives the impression of being very light and frothy but the verses are slower with Stewart's keyboards subtly changing the harmonic structure of the original to invoke a brooding atmosphere against which Gaskin's vocals sound more philosophical than fretful. The overall effect is not only harmonically different but also tonally more adult and thus less innocent and makes for gripping listening. Many people clearly agreed as it stayed at number one in the singles chart for four weeks in 1981. Would that all covers showed this degree of invention.

Some brave souls have attempted whole albums of covers of well-known songs. Tori Amos and Siouxsie and the Banshees have both released covers albums, but the prime example is probably 'Pin Ups' by David Bowie, who, at a high point in his career, had a lot to lose by getting it wrong. In it, material as challenging as Syd Barrett's 'See Emily Play' and the Who's 'I Can't Explain' are fearlessly given the rock chameleon treatment with, admittedly, some degree of success. To attempt new versions of such well regarded songs is almost akin to lunacy, but Bowie seems to have survived intact so fortune clearly favours the bold, but you can't help feeling that any lesser talent would have signed their commercial death warrant, so expansive is the graveyard labelled 'Covers'.

Having proposed that all covers must be different, I have just listened again to No Doubt's excellent cover of Talk Talk's 'It's My Life' and realised that the two are virtually note for note identical, so where does that leave me?

But popular music has always relied on cover versions of old songs. After all, a good song is a good song and if it is old enough, no one will remember the original. What is perhaps a little more humbling to discover is that the British beat boom of the early 1960s, led by the Beatles and bolstered by the Animals, the Hollies, the Searchers, Herman's Hermits and the rest of them, and which took

America by storm, was based to some extent on covers of American based songs. To find that Herman's Hermits' big hit of 1965, 'Silhouettes' was actually a cover of a song originally recorded by the American band, the Ronettes is a little deflating. Even the Beatles scored with a cover of the Marvelettes', 'Please, Mr Postman'.

But, of course, it is one thing to legitimately record a version of a song written by someone else and quite another to actually steal it and present it as your own work. In the early days of rock 'n' roll, the ownership of songs was open to some abuse as the wholesale lifting of material from little known American blues men by 1960s bands without acknowledgement attests, but in later years the problem of piracy and copyright evasion has become more pronounced. Even George Harrison was famously brought to book for using, unconsciously or otherwise, the melody from the Chiffons' hit, 'She's so Fine' to create his own best seller, 'My Sweet Lord' and there have been many other cases of alleged plagiarism of existing songs. With only twelve semitones in every octave, there must come a time when every combination has been tried and every melody has a counterpart.

Perhaps this is why the technology of sampling has been embraced with such fervour. It now seems easier to recycle music already written than to compose something new with the ever-present possibility that any newly written material may already exist anyway. Nevertheless, this is no real excuse to lift large chunks of past hits, wholesale, in order to give your own creation more commercial appeal. Frankly, I find the reworking of new melodies around old riffs from well-known songs desperately depressing, as it seems to parade a bankruptcy of ideas and only a willingness to succeed at any cost. Generally, it just makes me want to go out and buy the old song from which the sample has been lifted rather than the new cobbled together version, but this may be a symptom of my advancing age.

As Jane Austen would have recognised, it is a truth universally acknowledged that long-in-the-tooth music obsessives always recognise a crafty cover or sample when they hear it and then irritate younger generations, who are always unaware that any song can be recycled, by professing, "Of course, the original version by so-and-so was far superior." (See also – 'You can't hear what they're singing' and 'Is that a boy or a girl?')

Which, on the subject of aged rockers, brings us neatly to the great Radio 2 debate. It has become apparent that Radio 2 has come in for a certain amount of criticism for playing what some listeners have tended to refer to as, 'dreadful pop music'. Let's examine this assertion. The BBC launched Radio 1 in 1967 to replace a service once provided by the so-called Pirate radio stations, which had been finally extinguished by legislation, and that was, the broadcast of contemporary pop music to a predominantly under 30s audience. At the same time, Radio 2 was introduced and its remit appeared to be to provide musical entertainment for the older demographic. Judging by the content of the programmes broadcast, which tended to centre around 1940s big bands and 1950s balladeering from the likes of Frank Sinatra and his ilk, the target audience was probably in the 30–50 age bracket, assuming that these people would have be around 20 years of age when the style of music being played was in its prime. Presumably, those over the age of 50 were deemed to be Radio 4 listeners.

If this is a correct analysis, then today in 2005, assuming the same target age for its audience, Radio 2 should be playing music from the late 1970s punk era through the new romanticism and electropop of the 1980s to the urban rap of early 1990s. In other words, dreadful pop music. What it should not be playing is big bands from the 1940s and Frank Sinatra as this type of music now falls outside their target audience interests. What this actually boils down to is the fact that the original audience from 1967, now in the 70–90 age bracket, are still listening, expecting to hear their own favourites.

This is the eternal problem for all music playing radio stations. In fact, Radio 2 tries to cater for both age groups as the increased awareness of popular culture has penetrated far beyond the original target audience and may be the reason why the station seems to be caught out trying to be all things to all men. We seem to have come a long way from that old valve radio sitting in my grandmother's sitting room, permanently tuned to the Home Service. Today's grandmothers are far more discerning. Now, where did I put that Pat Boone LP?

One of the major benefits that technology has bestowed upon us is that it has given us almost unlimited access to the history of pop music, or, to put it another way, old songs. Not a month passes without a flood of re-releases of old material, either remastered and repackaged, or releases of material for the first time on CD, hitting the streets. No wonder the travelling minstrel went out of business, we have a comprehensive supply of music at our fingertips. Listening to music from your own childhood with adult ears is often a thought-provoking experience where the outcome usually falls into one of two categories, the 'Wow, that was great' category or the 'Whatever did I see in it?' category. As children, we tend to listen with uncritical ears where good and bad alike pass before us without analysis, but later on it should be all too obvious where the differences lie if it were not for the problem of over familiarity, which works to impair our critical faculties.

Recently, I found myself listening to 'San Francisco' on one of those hotchpotch compilations that pass for free CDs given away in the national press. This song is testament to John Phillips' (of Mamas and Papas fame) songwriting craft and was written for his old Journeymen colleague, Scott McKenzie but I've heard it a million times and it tends to just drift over me. However, on this occasion for some reason, I heard it with new ears, as if for the first time and it occurred to me what a great vocal performance Scott puts in. So much so, in fact, that I listened to it again and despite its familiarity, found it to be a very well written song performed by an accomplished singer. Oddly enough, this appreciation of its qualities had never really occurred to me before as I had carried around with me for 38 years my initial impression, formed when I was a largely uncritical 11 year old, that it was merely a run-of-the-mill single. And the more I thought about this the more I realised that these half formed impressions from long ago were probably suspect and needed revisiting.

I have tried the trick of attempting to listen to old recordings with new ears using various other songs from my past with sometimes startling results. I am not a great admirer of Diana Ross but having re-listened to her vocal performances in all those old 1960s Supremes singles, and here I'm thinking in particular about 'Stop, in the Name of Love' and 'You Keep me Hanging on', I have had to revise my opinion. In her youth, that breathy, pleading vocal quality allied to the somewhat anxious quality of the lyrics gave the Supremes a recognisably unique sound. Others have not fared quite so well. My collection of Mungo Jerry singles, of which I was once very proud, is now in danger of relegation to the second hand shop.

Every now and again I chance to hear 'Marrakesh Express' by Crosby Stills & Nash on the radio and immediately, without warning, I am transported back to my childhood sickbed in the house I was brought up in. I can see the wallpaper, my little bedside table with its pile of Superman comics and the gardens and fields beyond from my window. I can even smell the early autumn air and feel the watery sunshine. It was in the September of 1969 when I contracted the Mumps and had to stay in bed for a week or two before being certified fit for a return to school. The school cross country course ran along a muddy bridle path several hundred yards from the bottom of our garden and I could just see its course mapped out by hedgerows from my bedroom window. Even now I can feel the warm glow of relief that I felt then, knowing that my classmates would be trudging along that path without me.

As a consequence of my incarceration, I was allowed the family radio in my room to wile away the hours and for some reason this record was played constantly. It is not one of my favourites and it is for the very reason that I don't hear it very often that it remains permanently associated with those few weeks of my life now long gone. The sensory memories it invokes are incredibly powerful, involving not just mental images but smells and feelings too and I understand that this is not an uncommon experience for many people. But the linking of music with a certain historic event only really occurs when the piece of music is largely forgotten thereafter. This form of memory jogging rarely happens in relation to favourite songs, as they tend to be owned and consequently played constantly throughout your life and therefore lose the unique link with a single event. Although I can remember when I first heard various favourite songs, they are not joined specifically to that precise time and place as I have played them numerous times on other occasions, which has diluted the effect. But for 'Marrakesh Express', I still hold a unique set of memories that surprise me even now with their potency.

Whilst many songs attach themselves inextricably to happy memories, there are one or two that become forever linked with sadder times. For a short time after I left home in 1979, I shared a huge, slightly rundown detached house in Queens Park, northwest London, with 9 other people. We were a motley collection of twenty-somethings ranging from young professionals to University postgraduates and secretaries, but rubbed along tolerably well. During my time in residence there, a young girl called Debbie joined our ranks but to us older inmates, her sixteen-year-old effervescence was a touch wearing and together with her inability to pay her share of the rent, she struggled to fit in. It was also her habit to borrow my records without asking and return them in a less than pristine condition, which didn't help her case either.

One warm summer night, I arrived home from seeing Eric Clapton in concert at the Hammersmith Odeon only to find the house teeming with ambulance men and police officers. Having entered the house through the open French windows like some downmarket stage farce, I was confronted by my fellow housemates, who were collected in the sitting room, looking white faced and shocked. I soon found out why, as, being debarred from entering the hall, I espied through the partially open door a body bag emerging from Debbie's room carried by a team of ambulance men. It was then that the dreadful truth emerged – Debbie had committed suicide that afternoon by an overdose of sleeping pills. She had gone to her room, put my copy of Fleetwood Mac's 'Rumours' on her old auto-change record player and set it to play continuously while she took the pills and slipped away. It was only after the third or fourth repeat of the LP that, in irritation, anyone thought to go in to tell her to take the record off and her body was discovered.

I still have that copy of 'Rumours', scratched as it is, but never play it. It remains as a silent testimony to our collective guilt that we never made her more welcome.

Chapter Eleven

SCHOOL'S OUT

By the summer of 1974, my school career was all but over and the broad avenue of life stretched to a murky looking horizon. My first stumbling steps into a new phase in my life coincided with the release of that too-clever-by-half album 'Sheet Music' by 10cc. It's not that it is a bad album, far from it, but it did come at a time when attitudes towards this type of musically esoteric material was hardening and it foretells a sea change in the perception of rock music that would all end in tears when the punks arrived later in the decade. Not only was my life changing, but music was changing too.

Leaving school is a slightly scary, yet liberating feeling. Most people, thus liberated are faced either with a bleak future in work, or a bleak future in deferred work after a period in higher education and I was one of the latter. My first adult lifestyle choice was to spend a lazy summer doing nothing very much whilst waiting to go up to University in the autumn. But deferring work equated with deferring wealth so in order to help with my finances, which having given up my paper round were looking decidedly peaky, I looked to obtain temporary employment for a few months and fortunately, was given some help after a chain of events that started with that iconic band; the Doors.

Up to now, the Doors had not featured highly in my life. I had vaguely remembered a version of 'Light My Fire' by José Feliciano from about 1968 but hadn't really associated this acoustic version with Jim Morrison and Co until the Doors hit my radar in 1971 with the seminal 'Riders on the Storm'. This I first heard whilst listening to my transistor radio on the first fifteen coach to an away game one Saturday morning and it very nearly made me forget the forty minutes each way of legalised thuggery that constituted inter school rugby awaiting me, but not quite. I loved its loose, almost improvised feel and dark lyric and still do and on the strength of it decided to buy 'L A Woman', the album from whence it came.

It was at this point that my technological snobbery had got the better of me and I had opted to buy it on cassette, on the premise that this was the coming technology, rather than old-fashioned vinyl. Quite why I decided to do this still puzzles me as my only means of playing tapes was on a cheap W H Smith cassette player of indeterminate sound quality. But what was probably lurking in the back of my mind was the memory of a shining chrome plated box owned by my mate, Barry. Barry lived in a bungalow in a southern suburb of St Albans and even at this stage I should have read the signs. Clearly there was something about bungalows, recalling those days at my grandparents, that had an influencing effect on me and it was even money that some action would result from any proximity to this one.

On this occasion, Barry had invited me round to his house especially to impress me with his new toy, a combination of stereo amplifier and cassette deck complete with a pair of wood veneered loudspeakers and I *was* impressed. Barry whipped out one of his vast collection of Jimi Hendrix cassettes (he was a big fan) and inserted it into the machine. Jimi Hendrix is another that I have a conditional relationship with. Other than 'Electric Ladyland', I own no Hendrix albums and would not normally choose to sit down and listen to one. But watching him in action is another matter and I generally find him a mesmerising performer who exudes an air of utter confidence in his own ability, which translates into a strong feeling that anything is possible. To see him switching between rhythm and lead guitar as accompaniment to his own singing is astonishing but somehow, without the visual aid, his music is not half as engrossing.

Nevertheless, with the Hendrix tape ensconced in its metal body, the cassette player looked wonderful with its rotary controls and shimmering lustre and sounded great and it is probably for this reason alone that I opted to go down the cassette route. This decision, of course, would prove to be an utter disaster as all my tapes from that period are now completely unplayable and I have been forced to either replace them with CDs or lose them, and I never did buy that stereo cassette player.

Mind you, I wasn't the only one enthused by new technology. Another member of our inner circle, Derek, had made the unilateral decision that the future of rock 'n' roll lay in the 8 Track Cartridge, a much larger and more cumbersome version of the cassette tape designed specifically for car use as the enclosed tape was configured into an endless loop, thus negating the need for rewinding. Unfortunately for us, we hardly ever got to hear its benefits as Derek's aged Morris Traveller, in which the player was installed, was in a permanent state of overhaul. Any invitation to go out was usually met by the plaintive cry of 'I've got to do me brakes!' which soon became the male equivalent of the female 'I'm washing my hair!'

Thus unconvinced of the merits of the 8 Track Cartridge (and rightly so judging by its premature demise), 'L A Woman', on lurid green cassette, joined my collection but I was less than enthused with it and so it languished on my shelf for a few years until, at the time of which we speak, I sold it to my old school friend, Malcolm.

I had been friendly with Malcolm since our time in the sixth form when a crowd of us had whizzed around town in his beat-up Ford Anglia looking for likely pubs to patronise. Having ditched the Anglia on leaving school, his next proud ownership was a white Ford Cortina mark 1 GT (with green racing stripe, naturally), which he had 'modernised' to within an inch of its life, and he had recently installed a brand new tape based in-car stereo system – hence the need for tapes to play on it – and was happy to take 'L A Woman' off my hands for a small fee. During the Anglia days whilst we were sixth form students, we two had been the main exponents of the great Alquin hunt of '73. Alquin were a Dutch band comprising seven members who indulged in long complex and largely instrumental pieces of progrock and had featured on the TV programme of the day, The Old Grey Whistle Test. The album they were promoting was called 'The Mountain Queen' but could we find a copy anywhere? No. So it came to pass that any time we had a bit of free time at school, the two of us would screech out of school in the Anglia and roar (literally – the exhaust was a bit dodgy) over to a nearby town like Hatfield or Hemel Hempstead in a quest to track down a copy. Eventually, one was found in a small record shop in Stevenage and predictably the vinyl had a slight warp in the outer edge which looked like a roller coaster when playing but I hadn't the heart to make the journey back to replace it knowing that there was unlikely to be another copy in stock. But musically, it was worth it and I now have a replacement CD copy, which doesn't have the slight whooshing sound during the first few minutes.

As it turned out, Malcolm's father was an executive at an industrial works in nearby Welwyn Garden City that made flux rods and other unlikely products. It was he that secured three temporary holiday jobs for Malcolm, me and Terry in the stores and maintenance departments paying £25 per week – a small fortune to me, used to my paltry £1 a week. Nothing comes for nothing as we found out and the price for such riches was a 45-hour week over five and a half days with an eight o'clock start each morning. I had to be ready for seven o'clock every working day when Malcolm and Terry would arrive outside my door in the Cortina for the journey to Welwyn. Inevitably, our first order of business was to choose a tape to play in the car. The decision was not a complex one as the candidates were only twofold; my ex-copy of the Doors' 'LA Woman' now owned by Malcolm or his copy of 'Innervisions' by Stevie Wonder. I was not what you would call a Soul devotee, but I did like 'Innervisions' with its dark urban feel and catchy melodies and my vote tended to lean in that direction. These two tapes kept us amused for almost the whole three months that we worked at the factory before going our separate ways and they are both permanently engraved on my memory as a result. Our only relief was the addition of David Bowie's 'Diamond Dogs' and Eric Clapton's '461 Ocean Boulevard' late on in the day so that we could all sing 'I Shot the Sheriff' in cod Jamaican accents.

The factory itself was a cavernous grey shed that housed various factory lines and smelled of industry and oil. I was assigned to the maintenance department and spent my days helping to keep machines running and doing the sort of jobs no one else wanted, like reorganising the spares depot and painting everything from kerbstones to water gantries. The place had an air of inmates doing time and to a large extent they were doing just that – biding their time waiting for retirement. At least I had the luxury of knowing that in three months I would be gone but the early seventies trades union resentment was heavy in the air and the despair born of boredom was almost palpable. My abiding memory of that time is allied to Joni Mitchell's 'For the Roses' album, which I had just bought, and in particular the track 'Banquet' which bemoans the inequality of life and which seemed to fit my working environment like a glove. 'Who let the greedy in? And who left the needy out?' she demands in the final verse. And I didn't know.

I had initially come to Joni Mitchell via 'Court and Spark' after a long period of resistance caused by being told that I really ought to listen to her because I would like it. The fact that it was one of my schoolteachers, a fervent Joni and Pink Floyd fan that was doing the recommending didn't help matters either. I always hate to be told that I should listen to something or other anyway, but don't quite know why. Perhaps it is pride that I didn't discover whatever it was for myself or perhaps it is fear that I wouldn't like it and would then have to admit to my benefactor that I didn't. Either way,

I had stalled at Ms Mitchell's door for several years until I finally cracked and bought 'Court and Spark'. And, of course, I loved it. This then led to the purchase of earlier albums, 'Ladies of the Canyon' and then 'For the Roses'. The latter album is now one of my favourites, but at first I wasn't sure at all. On first hearing it presented itself as a little too earnest, a little too difficult melodically and a little too bare instrumentally after the more fully arranged 'Court and Spark'. But after a time the work took root in my mind and I found that I couldn't shift it. It was about this time that I started work in the factory and my daily tasks were undertaken to a soundtrack of this album in my head. The lyrics are some of the strongest she has ever written and have a resonance that is often unexpectedly moving. There are vignettes of life laid bare that are so acutely observed they play out before your eyes and so it was as I painted kerbstones during those long off summer days. There was undoubtedly the location factor coming into play again and the bleak setting of the factory coupled to the deeply philosophical lyrics made a lasting impression.

It is albums like this that gives lie to the assertion that all pop music is junk. This is an album that gives the listener not only musical pleasure but cause for thought and that can never be a bad thing. What it also did for Joni was to move her on a little from the folkie persona of her previous effort, 'Blue' to the slightly more pop/jazz stance adopted for the subsequent 'Court and Spark' where the transition to star is complete. With Tom Scott's LA Express as backing band her melodies on 'Court' take flight. The lyrics are still as cutting as ever but the pop/rock setting gives them a greater conviction. This album, in turn, acts as the bridge between 'For the Roses' and the subsequent 'The Hissing of Summer Lawns' where the journey to consummate musician is ended. On this album can be found folk, pop and jazz, as well as excursions into world music and gospel. Perhaps her best effort, it combines all her influences into a heady whole. Backed as before by Tom Scott, this leans towards free form jazz without losing the listener. The progression of maturity from 'Blue' to 'The Hissing of Summer Lawns' is one that few artists make in their whole career and puts Joni up amongst the greats, but also makes her a convincing ambassador for popular music that devotees like me can cite without embarrassment.

It was during those three months when I was working at the factory that I began to appreciate song lyrics in earnest and it was Joni Mitchell who pointed the way. Up to then and probably like most other people, I had considered the melody to be the primary engine in a song and the lyrics just there to make up the weight. I still believe this to be true, in principle, but it is the lyrical content that can turn a good song into a great one. There are two styles of lyric that I particularly like and those are lyrics that purport to say something about the human condition and lyrics that provide intriguing images without actually saying anything.

In the first category are writers like Bob Dylan, Joni Mitchell and Morrissey who aim to put across certain truths about life to their listeners. I have to confess at this point that I am not much for political posturing in pop music, feeling that there is no real place for propaganda in pop and therefore have always been a bit wary of the Red Wedge school of acts. But there are many writers who make a good job of imparting their own style of wisdom about life and love. Added to the list would be Paul Simon, Elvis Costello and Curt Cobain who have all, at some time, spoken to their respective age group in terms that are immediately recognisable.

As a subset of this category are the storytellers. These are the writers who love to construct novelettes such as Chris Difford and Glen Tilbrook's 'Up the Junction' from Squeeze's 'Cool for Cats' album chronicling the result of a doomed relationship. Another engaging storyteller is Julian Cope although most of his tales contain violence on a quite alarming scale. There's the story of 'Reynard the Fox' who meets a sticky end and the spoof road rage tale of

'Autogeddon Blues' where Cope imagines himself killing another driver by striking him on the head with a rock. All these tales are verging on music as theatre in much the same way that Jim Morrison and the Doors would use drama on stage to engage the audience in such pieces as 'The End', which does actually contain a spoken short story in the middle section. In my experience it is very common for lyrical stories to end badly or in an orgy of violence and in all these instances the music is used to heighten the drama of the story. Many folk singers also use the morbid story-telling style. Suzanne Vega tells the harrowing tale of the 'Queen and the Soldier' on her debut album and Maddy Prior has no end of gruesome outcomes lifted from traditional folk yarns in her solo work. Even Nick Cave ends up murdering Kylie Minogue in their duet 'Where the Wild Roses Grow'. The only drawback to story lyrics is that, like a book, once you know the ending it takes the shine off repeated listenings. Perhaps unjustly, this doesn't affect more opaque lyrics, which remain just as baffling after many plays.

In the second category I would tend to place certain songs rather than writers, as I'm not sure that lyric writers set out to write meaningless words but rather end up with something a bit obscure from time to time. But there is something very attractive about the combination of certain sounding words that form an impression without any sort of reality check. One of the best examples of this type of 'image' song is 'Whiter Shade of Pale' which contains some of the most memorable images in pop music, but is virtually meaningless as a whole. Somehow, the lack of meaning doesn't really detract from the beauty of the words and the images they conjure.

Another of my favourite image lyrics is a track called 'Shine On' by the House of Love from their eponymous 1990 album. In this song Guy Chadwick, the writer, alludes to isolation and the revealing of hidden talent (I think) but the images painted are vividly desolate, like the boy 'sitting lonely on a plastic chair'. This image is probably one of most eloquent I know and for me, the feeling of loneliness and isolation is summed up in its entirety by those five words. This is a good example of where an imaginative lyric raises a good song up to another level and produces a work of close to total perfection. The song comprises a well crafted melody in four distinct sections which marries a boisterous sing-a-long chorus to a softly dramatic verse and uplifting, harmony laden middle section and then adds a spirited guitar solo and loads of musical detail to flesh out the bones. Songs like this don't come along that often and is worth the price of the album alone.

Kate Bush is also not averse to surreal verbal imagery as the throwing shoes into lakes episode from her 'Hounds of Love' clearly demonstrates. If this type of verbal manoeuvring sounds suspiciously like poetry, don't be fooled. It isn't. Try reading the lyrics to most popular songs out loud and they sound ridiculous without the musical context. Conversely, genuine poetry does not make a good lyric – it is too stilted and too rigid in its metre. Song lyrics are a thing apart and for some reason the looser the better both rhythmically and grammar wise. Some of the best lyrics are hopelessly ungrammatical but have a natural conversational flow. Listen to 'My Way' to see how this works.

But for sheer mastery of language and wordplay for its own sake, look no further than 10cc, especially on their first four albums. The sort of lyrics they went in for had no real message but by the careful juxtaposition of certain words were able to create amusingly twisted meanings from everyday constructions. In the punk revolution that followed, such learnedness would be scorned but there is no doubt that there is much to be admired in its conception.

During my three months of toil, I had amassed a fair amount of cash. Having money was a foreign experience and at first, a little overwhelming. Initially I bought sensible items like a newly invented electronic calculator for my time at University. To someone who was completely at home with log tables this was high technology indeed and comprised a large bulky square of plastic with stiff buttons and a barely readable red LED display. But as time went on, my sights were focused on bigger and better things. There was a small shop near the railway station in Watford called KJ Leisuresound and it sold Hi Fi components like amplifiers and turntables. I had passed it many times and looked in its windows longingly, but now with means to dream, I looked again with renewed interest. The shop also offered a mail order service and by the end of my three-month working life I had amassed sufficient funds to purchase my first real stereo sound system. I hesitate to use the words High and Fidelity because in truth the components I bought were adequate rather than esoteric. They comprised the ubiquitous Garrard SP25 turntable with Goldring cartridge, a cheap Japanese Teleton amplifier and a pair of KJ's own brand loudspeakers and I was immensely pleased with them.

By now, the music bug had mutated into its advanced form whereby I would be forced to spend the next twenty years buying bigger and better equipment until the demands of a family caused a halt. All this enthusiasm for a better sound involved the reading of all the monthly glossy Hi Fi magazines and countless trips to specialist equipment shops to strain to hear the difference between more and more expensive gear. But if you are a music lover, it is a hugely satisfying experience to listen to it on equipment that portrays it in a rhythmically and tonally correct way, with every strand properly separated and presented. Even now, I would never have it any other way.

By the end of the summer, I was ready to move on to pastures new and prepared to leave home for the first time to sample the delights of higher education. By this time my record collection was becoming large enough to consider taking it an impossibility. Also, the thought of uprooting my brand new stereo was not appealing and so set about transferring many of my favourite LPs onto tape with a view to taking a box of cassette tapes and my radio cassette player.

Thus prepared, I awaited the start of my new life with a little more confidence.

Chapter Twelve

A WOMAN OF HEART AND MIND

Whilst I admire musical talent greatly and have a moderate understanding of technical dexterity, there is one area that often causes me problems of appreciation and it is the singing voice. Call me a Philistine if you must but I just cannot get to grips with a trained operatic voice at all. I can understand the work and the effort that has gone into producing such tone, sustain and accuracy, the endless hours of practice and self-sacrifice but to me it has the effect of homogenising the voice so that everyone ends up sounding exactly the same, minimising any sort of individual personality. Compare this to most untrained voices, and in this respect I am not being critical, belonging to the majority of popular singers and what you invariably hear is bags of personality at the expense of some musical accuracy. I know that I would much rather listen to Siouxsie Sioux's ever so slightly flat delivery or Jarvis Cocker's blokish storytelling or even David Byrne's tortured delivery than a host of classical singers as I know instantly whom I am listening to and, more importantly, I can hear their soul. And this is the nub as far as I am concerned. If I cannot hear the singer's personality coming through then neither is there emotion. Debbie Harry is not one of the world's great singers, in a technical sense, but her larger than life personality is constantly evident and we are, accordingly, hanging in there with her every note of the way.

This is not to say that pop singers are not good technically as, for example Abba's Agnetha and Frida demonstrate. Try singing 'Dancing Queen' and see how far you get before you are straining to clear those high notes in the chorus, yet those two manage it effortlessly. In fact, the tune spans about an octave and a half, more than enough for most people. There are other numerous examples of competence, so it is not ability that offends my ear, but there is something about ability stretched to the limit and its effect of squeezing all accent and character out that really makes me despair.

There are various examples of singers whose voice you would not describe as perfect, yet as a direct result of this 'disability' benefit from exhibiting an immediately recognisable character. In the list would be idiosyncratic vocalists such as Bob Dylan, Mick Jagger, Rod Stewart, Tom Waites, Björk and Kate Bush. All these people have a recognisable style that sets them apart from the crowd thus aiding self-publication. Also, I have never been able to fathom why some accents are immediately noticeable in a person's singing voice and not others. Why, for example are we able to immediately recognise the strong Scottish burr of the Proclaimers, yet not the similar accents of Midge Ure or Jim Kerr? Cerys Matthew's Welsh intonation is also obviously apparent but you wouldn't peg either the Stereophonics or even Tom Jones to be of the same nationality without very careful listening.

Perhaps it is because many vocalists imitate our cousins from the far side of the Atlantic in their singing voice. Certainly the short 'a' sound, as in 'baton' is easier to sing in a word like 'dance', rather than the longer 'dahnce', but it all gets a bit ridiculous when 'I'm' becomes 'Ah'm'. There are only a few singers that sing in a true English accent and one of them is Peter Gabriel. It is almost comically noticeable that he will always sing 'cahn't' rather than the shorter 'can't' and the aforementioned 'dahnce' rather than 'dance'. It sounds so odd because virtually nobody else does it yet it is the way that most English people, at least in the south, pronounce these words. Then there is the folk singer Kate Rusby, who is a good example of how dialects show through in the singing voice. Hailing from Barnsley, her flat Yorkshire vowels are apparent in her singing voice and this gives a certain credibility to the sort of folk songs she tends to favour. Folk tradition often emanates from the working class and her genuine northern accent gives a real credence to the sentiments expressed, even though she may not consider herself to be working class now.

Ever since that defining moment when Curved Air's 'Back Street Luv' entered my life, I have had an affinity for female vocalists, especially fronting a male dominated rock band. Back in 1971 there were very few bands with this configuration although Jefferson Airplane and Renaissance spring notably to mind. Since that time every band and his dog seems to have a girl vocalist. Through my preference, I seem to have amassed examples of 45 such bands from Abba to Evanescence. The punk/new wave era stoked up this burgeoning trend with the likes of Blondie, Altered Images, The Passions, Penetration, The Shop Assistants, The Slits and Siouxsie and the Banshees all surfacing at that time. Subsequently the list expands through All About Eve, Dubstar, The Cardigans, Garbage, Portishead, St Etienne, The Sundays, Voice of the Beehive and so on and on.

Quite why this construct should be so popular is open to debate, but I dare say that in most media sex sells and music is no different when it comes to putting a pretty girl in range of the consumer. Nevertheless, there is something else and my guess is that it is connected to the distribution of pitch within a piece of music. I am no recording engineer, but it seems to me that female vocals, being slightly higher in pitch than most male counterparts, do not clash with the natural ranges of other instruments and therefore have a clarity of their own which projects them out from the mix of sounds that constitutes the whole piece. It is interesting to note that in heavy metal bands, where there is, almost by definition, a lot of noise going on, male vocalists sing in a high-pitched or falsetto voice in order to make themselves heard. AC/DC, Led Zeppelin and latterly, The Darkness all use this device to some effect. This seems to suggest that a higher vocal pitch is required where the band is of the more energetic type as it helps make the vocals stand out.

Blondie were undoubtedly the best example, combining as they did, a strong female personality with a dynamic punk inspired male band. It is all too easy to remember Blondie as a pure pop band with an attractive singer, but their strength lay not only in Debbie Harry's charismatic presence but also in the well-drilled and aggressive band behind her. This was a band that had emerged from the gritty New York punk scene but had retained the energy and dynamics of punk and had put it to good use in their radio friendly singles. Have another listen to 'Hanging on the Telephone' to experience how its breathtakingly tight rhythm, driven by Clem Burke's immaculate drumming gets your pulse racing from the first few seconds and never lets go. Blondie were essentially a loud and raucous club band that had diverted their inherent energy into producing tight exciting pop records. Certainly, I find that the combination of a genuinely innovative rock band and a female voice, especially one where the personality and/or accent of the singer is allowed to flourish over technique, is one of the great pleasures of popular music.

And all this explains why I am no fan of either Whitney Houston or Mariah Carey. Perhaps it is a little unfair to single out these two divas but, in my opinion, they do represent a school of singing that glamorises technical ability above all else. Admirers tell me that they have soulful voices, but I can't hear it above the forceful blast of sound and flurry of notes that hide any melody struggling to assert itself. If the overblown rendition of Dolly Parton's 'I Will Always Love You' is anything to go by Whitney Houston and her ilk will never feature in my collection. Obviously, this is a personal preference but there are too many other women that I would rather to listen to before I would even consider them. In fact, and you may be surprised by this, I have a list of them and I have named my favourites; the Anti-Whitney League. Here are just four of them in no particular order.

1. Shirley Manson

Shirley and I go back a long way. Not personally, you understand as I have never met her, but she was the subject of my most spectacularly correct bit of talent spotting ever. Sometime in the early 1980s, I went to a gig headlined by Aztec Camera with a bunch of mates who were into the Roddy Frame school of song-writing. Unusually for us, we stayed away from the bar long enough to witness the support act, a band called Goodbye Mr McKenzie, whom I had half an ear to whilst rudely conversing over their entire set. I could hear that they were fronted by a male vocalist, but every now and then there was a female voice that contributed backing vocals and the occasional lead line. Whilst not exactly riveting, the band had something about them and it was that female voice. Whenever she had a line or two to sing, the music seemed to lift a little and when she had finished her bit, my interest waned. Out of the corner of my eye I spotted her – a very young, rather odd-looking girl skulking about in the shadows. During the interval, the conversation turned to the merits of Goodbye Mr McKenzie and I recklessly proposed a plan of action that I thought would help them and that was to ditch the lead singer and put the girl up front. I even went as far as to say that she would be a future star. This was greeted with the usual withering disdain as my last twenty-odd tips had fallen on distinctly stony ground and it was promptly forgotten by all. The years passed by, life carried on and I, too, had forgotten but then, some *ten years* later, I was staggered to learn that the female vocalist of a new exciting band called Garbage was none other than the odd looking girl, now revealed as Shirley Manson and as of today, she is a genuine star. Apparently, the rest of the band had picked her out whilst watching MTV when her band at the time, Angelfish was playing. Well, you've got to be right once in your life and I am ridiculously pleased that she made it and not just because I tipped her all those years ago, but because she is a genuinely emotive singer of great accuracy. Listen to her singing live and you will never hear a duff note despite the often mildly discordant content of Garbage's material. Like all good singers, she never seems to have to fight against the band but will often sing quite softly to add dynamic range to a song. Her soft Scottish intonation is also full of character and helps to convey the wry irony that comprises some of her best lyrics, such as in 'I'm Only Happy When it Rains' in a way only Morrissey can match.

2.   Julianne Regan

Julianne Regan fronted an outfit called All About Eve in the late 1980s and 1990s who, as a result of their origins were often pigeon-holed with the goth crowd. This was not strictly accurate but the band certainly managed to produce a few longer pieces that could be described as having gothic grandeur. During their tenure, their calling card was generally a fine ear for producing music that contained a multitude of rock dynamics ranging from all out grunge to lilting acoustic whimsy, often in the same piece. All this was overlaid with Julianne's pure, crystalline, rather posh sounding voice. This combination of band and voice rather intrigued me, as the result often resembled what you might imagine Celia Johnson circa 1945 fronting Iron Maiden would sound like. Julianne also has a very fine sense of harmony and her backing vocals were always carefully constructed and beautifully intricate. Their second album, 'Scarlet and Other Stories' was produced at a time when, by her own admission, her emotional life was on the verge of collapse, yet it is an album of eternal beauty. It seems that great albums are always born of the pain of disintegrating relationships, Fleetwood Mac's 'Rumours' and Joni Mitchell's 'Blue' are other well known examples and those forged from relative contentment turn out to be insufferably smug. We respond to others' distress in a way that bonds us to their work and the retention of Sinead O'Connor's spontaneous tear in her unblinkingly intimate video for

'Nothing Compares 2 U' is testament to this power. In their heyday, my wife and I attempted to see Julianne and the boys play at London's Royal Albert Hall but, due to demand, could only obtain standing tickets at the very top of the Hall, about a million miles from the stage and probably behind a pillar. On the way to the venue, on a reckless whim, I did something I'd never done before nor have I done since; I bought tickets from a tout. Admittedly, they were very good seats but having parted with both my existing tickets and a fair amount of cash, the transaction left a nasty taste in the mouth. Inside the Hall, we searched for our seats and found them right at the front near to the stage in an area that had 'Tout's Corner' written all over it. The venue was absolutely packed except for the few near empty rows where our seats were and we edged into them with some embarrassment, ensuring that our gaze was to the front so as not to inadvertently catch the eyes of any of our fellow punters and probable tout ticket holders, sitting close to us. The concert was fine, but the edge had been taken off it by thoughts of lining the pockets of the underworld. It was akin to eating a whole plateful of cream cakes; irresistible at first, still reasonably good fun to do, but leaving you with a slightly sick feeling afterwards. Never again.

3.   The Sugababes

The Sugababes comprise three of the finest singers you could hope to hear in Heidi Range, Mutya Buena and Keisha Buchanan. Although they have now experienced international chart success, this talented trio were cruelly caught up in and initially sunk by the TV talent show phenomenon that has comprised Pop Idol, Fame Academy and the rest. In late 2000, whilst the nation was holding its breath waiting to discover which individuals would make up the first talent show band, Hear'say, the teenaged Sugababes were launching their own career. Predictably, in the glare of the Hear'say novelty, they stumbled and were eventually dropped by their record company. At this stage, they may have disappeared forever like so many before them but luckily for us, Island records picked them up in 2002 and they haven't looked back, but there is a rather alarming lesson to be learned here from this cameo. Defenders of the TV reality show products argue that talent is brought to the public eye and this may be so, but apart from Will Young and Girls Aloud, virtually none of the various winners have endured. Hearsay lasted barely twelve months before they imploded in a wave of public indifference and during their run, the nation's eyes had been diverted from some bigger talents. Intriguingly, Liberty X, formed by the losing contestants, has enjoyed a better career away from the harsh winners' spotlight. It may be argued that the public who vote for these hopefuls are primarily television watchers, not music lovers and are therefore more interested in the excitement of the show that spawns the product than the product itself and if this is so, real talent is always in danger of being overlooked and may never have the break they deserve. Thankfully, in the case of the Sugababes, they survived and we now have the sublime 'Caught in a Moment' from their cunningly titled third album 'Three' to savour forever. With its gentle hip-hop beat, swirling synthesisers and understated guitar lines, it is the perfect setting for some of the most beguiling singing I have heard for a long time. I shall be enjoying this long after the talent show bands have disappeared.

4.   Sarah Blackwood

In the mid 1990s, ex DJ Steve Hillier and guitarist Chris Wilkie formed Dubstar, whose mission statement was to provide club-style electro dance/pop with melody for the masses. Their only problem was that they didn't have a singer and by association a band focus. Enter Sarah Blackwood, student, singer and band focus. Bands like Dubstar and in particular, M People gave me a small glimmer of hope that it wasn't too late for us oldies to make it in the music world. These bands had been formed by men that were either dangerously close to, or on the wrong side of, thirty with the idea that they would provide the songs but hide their identity behind a much younger (and preferably female) singer in order to create a fresh new image. And to a large degree this approach worked. Today, this anonymity is out of fashion and singers are drafted in where necessary under titles such as 'DJ Jeanius W Righter feat. Ann E Singer'. It is noticeable how many successful bands contain at least one person who has a grasp of musical construction that allows the rest to function and the age or identity of that person scarcely matters. Think Alan Price in the Animals or Graham Nash in the Hollies. The Sex Pistols are also a prime example of the 'power within' syndrome. Their power within was Glen Matlock, their original bass player. It was arguably his musical understanding that created the structure for all their early successful singles. When he left and was replaced by Sid Vicious, their songwriting collapsed like pack of cards. M People already had their power within in Mike Pickering and they recruited Heather Small, a hugely charismatic singer, as their band focus. Dubstar took Sarah Blackwood on board, who was a more enigmatic vocalist. Sarah's style is a cool, articulate yet semi spoken singing approach which, given the right material, is extremely effective. The fact that her singing voice accentuates her Halifax accent is also a plus in her favour. There is a track on their second album called 'Ghost' where the lyrics have Sarah talking to a recently deceased partner and it is here that her unique style is shown at its best. The vocal line is sung, but has a spoken cadence about it that makes the listener feel that she is speaking to them directly as if in conversation. Given the melancholy subject matter of the song and the beautifully mournful melody, the effect is powerfully emotive and I have been known to mysteriously get something in my eye whilst listening to it.

Having said all this I do not wish to give the impression that I hate all male singers. Those that have thrilled me at sometime or other include Morten Harket of A-ha with his remarkable soaring voice, REM's sensitive Michael Stipe and most recently, Tom Chaplin of Keane, whose pure tones I could listen to all day. My personal standard for male vocalists has become known as 'The Queen Test' and was instigated during the Queen memorial concert for Freddie Mercury. As the saying goes, you never know what you have until it is gone and hearing a variety of well known singers attempt Queen songs on that day made me realise what tremendous power and range Freddie's voice had. Virtually everybody struggled to match the sheer exuberance of his delivery except one who coped in comfortable style. Yes, you've guessed, it was George Michael. George was a revelation that day, outperforming all his peers with effortless renditions of Queen classics. And this was not a one-off because having heard him sing covers of Elton John's 'Don't Let the Sun Go Down on Me' and others there is no doubt that George is possessed of one of the finest voices of his generation. Which makes it such a tragedy that his own material is so dire of late. The only other person to pass the Queen test so far has been Robbie Williams, who although not having the same quality of vocal chords as George Michael gets by on sheer exuberance alone. David Bowie gets an honorary membership for 'Under Pressure' but until I hear anybody else attempt a Queen song in earnest (no, not you, Five), I shall be putting the list into abeyance.

There is one instance where the appreciation of any half decent singing voice is enhanced and that is hearing a backroom songwriter give a performance of his or her own songs. I remember seeing a television documentary of the great Diane Warren where she sings one or two of her own songs as work in progress and to hear her struggling with the melodic range of her own creation is a strange experience. I always find it odd that someone who can create such wonderful songs cannot actually communicate their beauty. It takes someone like LeAnn Rimes to show us how good they are.

In a similar vein, there was a reality programme shown in 1998 entitled 'Jobs for the Boys' where comedians Gareth Hale and Norman Pace were tasked with writing a Eurovision song entry. For most of the programme, we were treated to their stumbling attempts to create a melody and lyrics and then perform it in faltering voices but it was not until the completed song was handed to one or two well known singers to try out did their effort suddenly blossom into a reasonable song. In particular, in the hands (or should that be vocal chords) of Katrina Leskanich, of Katrina and the Waves fame and an extremely accomplished singer, the song took on the identity of a real contender with depth and drama and in fact, the song only narrowly missed being chosen to be represented in the final eight songs from which that year's UK entry in the contest would be picked.

I have tried to put forward the case for the relatively untrained voice in this chapter, but there is a downside and that is that such voices seem to fare less well with the passing of time. Having just witnessed both Morten Harket and Annie Lennox performing at the various Live8 concerts, there is no doubt that the edge has come off their prodigious talent leaving them as mere mortals again.

So what is it about the human voice that causes us to like or dislike, deride or praise, to rise in defence or belligerent attack? Is it just taste or is there something else at work here? It is probably to do with biology and those tiny bones in our inner ear, the names of which I've forgotten, and the fact that they are different in every one of us, making our hearing unique. This is probably just as well or we'd all be fervent Jamelia fans and Jennifer Lopez wouldn't get a look in. There again...

Chapter Thirteen

LIVING IN ANOTHER WORLD

Listening to records and watching bands mime on television is all very well, up to a point. But there is no substitute for watching and listening to music being played live. The Musicians' Union have long espoused the slogan, 'Keep Music Live' and who's to say that they are not wrong?

So it was, in the early 1970s, that I started the slow descent into deafness and went to see bands play live. The St Albans area was well endowed with venues and choice varied between a myriad of music pubs, the Students' Union at Hatfield Polytechnic (now the something-or-other University) and the more upmarket town hall type destinations at Hemel Hempstead, Dunstable and St Albans itself. Ticket prices were usually a bit steep for a man with a paper round but entry at the door on the night was commonplace unless a very big name was playing.

In retrospect, my first ever gig could have been an awe inspiring experience had it not been for the interference of that most unpredictable of human attributes: sex. I had gleaned from the NME that my first love, Curved Air, was to play at Hatfield Polytechnic and in high anticipation, had eagerly secured tickets for Terry and me. All was going smoothly as the due date drew near until suddenly, the week before, two rogue factors entered the equation. First, I was devastated to learn in the music press that, in true Twin Towers style, both Francis Monkman, the synthesiser guru and Florian Pilkington-Miksa, the drummer had left the band. This was bad enough, but their replacements included a guitarist, the very omission of which had set them apart. Hard on the heels of this setback came a second. Terry dropped the bombshell that disrupts most teenage friendships – he'd acquired a girlfriend, Nickey, and she would have to come as well. With a mixture of envy and annoyance, I duly purchased another ticket and hoped for the best. But there was more to come. What had not been disclosed was that Nickey's father insisted on taking us and would then pick her up at no later than 10.00 pm and that meant we would have to leave too. As it turned out Curved Air didn't start their set until about 9.30 pm so we were forced to leave after the first 30 minutes, much to my irritation. Fortunately, my friendship with Terry endured and I was not deterred from attending further gigs by this experience, but it was still one hell of an initiation.

With ticket prices beginning to accelerate in the inflationary 70s, gig attendance on my part dwindled. So when I secured a place at University for the autumn of 1974, I was heartened by the fact that I could see a three-year stretch of unfettered band watching at rock bottom prices coming my way. How little I knew.

Unfortunately, by 1974, the age of progressive rock was on the wane. Yes had released 'Tales from Topographic Oceans' to almost universal derision, Jethro Tull had gone off in a sulk following a similar panning of their 'Passion Play' and the rest were playing longer and longer pieces in larger and larger stadiums. It was all becoming too overbearing. The difficulty was that their bright young replacements in the singles market were the irritating glam rock pioneers of Mud, Sweet, the Rubettes and Gary Glitter and in the albums market there was an American invasion of slick, bland, middle of the road acts such as the Eagles, Steely Dan and Bob Seeger. There were a few saving graces like Roxy Music, Bowie, 10cc and perhaps Slade, but in most respects it was dire. And this state of affairs continued into 1975 and 1976. In 1977, just as punk was sweeping away swathes of this dross, I graduated and went home. My three years in the seeing live bands for next to nothing zone had been neatly positioned between the end of progressive and the start of punk or, in other words, the worst three-year period in musical history, bar none.

One day, during my first term, I saw a poster advertising Supertramp's 'Crime of the Century' tacked up in the union bar. The graphic it contained looked like someone had been locked in the sewers for some unspecified time and was desperate to escape. Having heard their single 'Dreamer', I could understand why; it had one of those non-specific rhythms that were neither one thing nor the other. I have to say that my relationship with this band has been one of grudging tolerance rather than enjoyment, and despite the fact that I own both 'Crime of the Century' and 'Breakfast in America' and have mellowed somewhat towards them, I just cannot seem to like them unreservedly. As well as advertising the album, the poster also urged us to see them live at the students' union the following week. Normally, I would not have countenanced a visit, but persuaded by a few others, with whom I had struck up a friendship, I found myself a spectator at my first low cost gig. I cannot even begin to pin down what it was that failed to involve me but somehow, like 'Dreamer', I always found myself waiting for each song to get started only to find that it was virtually finished. It was this feeling that nothing was ever resolved that began to irritate me and by the end I hated them with a vengeance. It wasn't really how I had envisaged my concert career at University would commence, and I hoped for better things.

Aside from sex, students in their first year worry about two things; making friends and hunger. The first had been partially alleviated by making all first year students share a room thus providing a live-in friend and the second was usually remedied by a visit to either the nearby chip shop or baker. The Hall of Residence I had been assigned to comprised a white stucco ex-hotel on a corner plot which served as the main focus with bar, common room and dining area and three adjacent residential houses. A newly constructed purpose built block of study bedrooms had been built in the area that used to be the gardens of these houses. I was to share a room in one of the houses, a tall rather dilapidated Victorian villa converted for student use with two large shared rooms on each floor. My room mate, Glen, was a mathematician from Birmingham and in the great tradition of Brummie heavy metal types such as Ozzy Osbourne, had arrived with an armful of heavy rock LPs including Hawkwind, Led Zeppelin, Blue Oyster Cult, Budgie and Pavlov's Dog and an old autochange record player. This rather put my slightly more demure collection of taped albums in the shade, but having listened politely to a selection of my stuff on my small cassette player, he rather surprisingly declared an interest in my Curved Air and Fanny albums, and so we bumped along companionably for the first year.

We solved our hunger crisis by buying cheap white loaves from the baker across the road and settling down to eat the whole loaf in one sitting by tearing pieces off with our bare hands like two starving cavemen. But the real issue here was not the fact that we were dying of hunger but what music to play whilst we were devouring the spoils? What we needed was some music sympathetic to bread devouring. Somehow, sitting down to eat with Led Zeppelin's 'Black Dog' or 'Four Sticks' blaring in the background didn't seem quite right and after much lively debate during which time most of our respective albums were rubbished, the only other album that we could both agree on was the Beatles' rather ponderous 'Let it Be', so this somewhat uninspiring album would accompany our feasts for the best part of a year. I still cannot hear 'Get Back' or 'Across the Universe' now without feeling a slight pang of hunger.

In every life experience there is something to be gained and my association with Glen brought forth an interest in Blue Oyster Cult's debut LP. This would be played almost daily and displayed a fine mastery of melody behind the heavy rock façade, unusual in the genre at that time and certainly unusual in the rest of his collection. By bunging this on the record player before he arrived, I could stave off another bout of Hawkwind's 'Brainbox Pollution' or something indecipherable from Budgie for twenty minutes or so and for that alone it deserves a place in my hall of fame.

Academic terms lasted for thirty weeks of the year and in between terms I would return home. During those periods, I used to make a point of frequenting the Beehive pub in St Albans where, in an upstairs room, a folk club was held once a week. The Beehive was not large by any standards and the accommodation was not what one would call roomy, hence early attendance usually paid dividends by way of securing a seat for the proceedings. Each week a couple of club regulars would play and then the floor was thrown open to guests. These would range from the semi professional to the nervous first timer but irrespective of technique and even talent, they were always interesting. There is nothing quite like sitting in front of an audience with just a guitar and your own unamplified voice to bring music down to its grass roots. There is an inherent honesty in such gatherings that is a solemn reminder of what music is all about, away from the hype and crassness of the commercial world. To hear a well structured and well presented song in such an intimate environment where the singer is passionate about their subject can be a profoundly moving experience and not one that I liked to miss if I could help it.

There is also something comfortingly historic about music that has been handed down through the generations over centuries that binds you to your own past, whatever your nationality. Like nursery rhymes that have survived for hundreds of years, traditional folk songs tell us about past events and personalities, about politics and social change in a way that it is not always possible to grasp from other sources. Songs written today about mundane events are sure to be just as interesting to future generations as those written about the industrial revolution are to us. Anyway, the point was that I managed to see some cheap live gigs and enjoyed them, even if they weren't exactly what I was expecting nor in the place I was expecting.

Also, as a budding guitarist I was interested to watch others play and became interested in their finger picking styles. I had become friendly with a fellow student named Brett who was a real whiz at folk finger picking and could play all manner of impressive blues and folk pieces. He lent me some sheet music of a sample of pieces by the English folk guitarist John Renbourn and I subsequently spent a huge amount of time trying to play some of the easier pieces for myself, as they sounded so good when he played them. This became a real labour of love as the fingering patterns were not the same as normal chords and required a back to basics approach that was initially incredibly frustrating. I never did get to play half the pieces I chose and even those I managed to stumble through became all too easily forgotten if not played regularly. Consequently, I can no longer play any of them, which is a great disappointment to me. I wish I had the determination to continue trying to master this style but I fear a lack of talent is the millstone that will ensure my ultimate failure.

This sudden awakening to the merits of folk music sent me scuttling back to check out the likes of Steeleye Span, whom I had derided at length in my capacity as school rock bore some years earlier. In particular, I became a great fan of their 'Parcel of Rogues' LP which contains some inventively reworked versions of ancient folk songs, some dating back to the 1600s. They also had the good fortune to have secured the talents of Maddy Prior, one of the finest folk singers this country has ever produced. Although dangerously close to that finger in the ear style of voice so beloved of folk singer parodies, her interpretations of traditional folk have a reassuringly English sound to them that brings their history to life in the modern world. In a similar vein, I have enjoyed the soft intonation of Irish singer, Mary Black and more recently, the music of Kate Rusby whose pure English rose voice is another welcome change after so much trans Atlantic mimicry.

It was about this time that I made my first tentative steps towards trying to write my own songs and consequently discovering that it was a bit more complicated than I had supposed. I had naively imagined that each song was the product of a single musical idea, that is 'the tune'. On reflection I realised that in reality you needed a verse and a chorus but on further investigation and after careful listening to some of my favourite writers, found to my horror that most good songs usually contained three separate melodic ideas and in the case of the better ones, four ideas. I call the former ABC songs and the latter ABCD songs. The various sections are:

a) The verse
b) The bit that links the verse and the chorus
c) The chorus
d) The extra bit that's different from all the above

As an example of how this works, think of Kate Bush's chart topping song, 'Wuthering Heights'. In this carefully crafted ABCD song there are four distinct sections as described above, each with a new melodic idea (and some with a new key, but that needn't concern us here). The following lines indicate the beginning of each section:

a) The verse: 'Out on the wiley windy moors we'd roll and fall in green'
b) The link from verse to chorus: 'Bad dreams in the night. They told me I was going to lose the fight'
c) The chorus: 'Heathcliff, it's me, Cathy come home, I'm so cold, let me in your window'
d) The extra section: 'Oh, let me have it. Let me grab your soul away'

This made song-writing bloody hard work as you had to think up four separate ideas that were all different yet were compatible with each other and all incredibly catchy into the bargain – and I hadn't even got around to finding the harmonic chords or writing the lyrics. This is where an appreciation for the teenaged Kate and all those who write songs began to grow. When you listen to a good song, you are hardly aware of the separate parts that make it up because there is an organic flow to the thing where each new part follows on naturally from the last. There is an eternal dichotomy that dictates that songs that you can hum on first hearing are made to sound so simple that they appear easy to create but in reality are usually the hardest.

My very first song was thus very short. It had only a verse and a chorus, a few chords and some of the worst lyrics imaginable. There was no getting away from it, if I was to spend all my energy on music writing, I needed a lyric writer but finding one would mean admitting to someone that I was trying to write songs and they would expect to hear them, so I knocked that idea on the head fairly rapidly. A more cunning approach was to peruse a copy of the university magazine, which often contained verse or short poems. In this underhand manner, I managed to pilfer lyrics for two or three songs before the magazine ceased publication. One such unknowing contributor was a fellow student, an individual named Keith, of whom more later in this chapter. This resulted in my first few attempts having rather ridiculous, flowery lyrics, rather unsuited to popular songs, but it helped me to get started in what was to become a favourite pastime. Eventually, I came to write lyrics as well and within a few years I had filled a music manuscript book with mainly half developed songs. When I look at them now there are about two that I would put my name to and the rest exhibit varying degrees of dreadfulness. But there's nothing like doing something yourself to appreciate those who do it well, is there?

During my second and third years, I had a room to myself and eventually gave in to the need to have both my stereo and all my records with me. This meant having to hike three large boxes of records and all the components of my stereo system from home to car and then from car to room six times a year, but it was worth it despite the odd complaint from neighbouring rooms. The advantage of having my own room was that I was able to spend more time writing songs and this I did for the remainder of my academic career. But I still wanted to make them into something more than just a vocal line and a guitar accompaniment but this would not happen for some time.

Of course, the alternative to writing songs was playing in a band but this concept was always far too scary a proposition to contemplate. Nevertheless, there was an incident that almost propelled me into the limelight before I knew what was happening. Living in Hall at the time of this episode was a student named Nick, a red-haired wiry individual who was a fellow rock bore of previously unimagined proportions. He owned a record collection of staggering magnitude and diversity and knew everything there was to know about the genre. This was the person, who, when I casually mentioned that I liked Deep Purple's double live album, 'Made in Japan', countered loftily with the withering, 'I only *ever* buy studio albums....' right.

He also did a bit of DJ-ing on the side and played a mean guitar into the bargain. One evening I came across him and a few of his mates attempting to play cover versions of well-known standards. Amongst his makeshift band, I was rather taken aback to find Andy, well known to me as someone who had recently made a split-second decision to become a rock star after listening to Roxy Music's 'Love is the Drug' for several weeks in a darkened room. A more unlikely candidate for stardom you could not imagine, but a poor quality guitar had been purchased from the local second-hand shop and here he was, taking his first faltering steps on the road to fulfilling his dream. The only problem was; he couldn't play. After several tentative minutes, he passed the guitar over and challenged me to, 'Here, have a go!'

In the spirit of camaraderie and having ascertained the chords from Nick we jammed around an old Buddy Holly song and against my rhythm playing, Nick suddenly took flight with one of those tumbling Chet Atkins style rock 'n' roll solos. It was a magical moment and at the end we just stared at each other before he stated quite firmly, 'Right, with a bit more practice we can enter the student band competition next month!'

What? Me?!

Andy was not best pleased at suddenly finding himself sacked from a band that hadn't even been formally created and I felt as if I had been catapulted into a dreadfully tricky social situation clutching a borrowed guitar and without an escape route. Luckily, after the euphoria had ebbed away the planned band idea was dropped and Andy got his guitar back. So far as I know, he didn't make it as a rock star, but then, neither did any of us.

Nevertheless, our Hall of Residence *was* represented in the great band competition by the shambolic and utterly chaotic, Metabolic Junk Boyz, a creation of the aforementioned Keith. Keith was what was generally described as a 'character', complete with wildman looks and extrovert personality, who used to entertain the dinner queue from a convenient table top with renditions of his two favourite songs, 'Knocking on Heaven's Door' and 'Horse with No Name' on his very nearly correctly tuned guitar. He also wrote odd poetry and behaved in a way that caused most people to avoid him. In this respect he was definitely a rock star in the making, being utterly eccentric, almost talented and a prime candidate for the Barking Mad category of artists. Around him, he collected a bevy of like minded almost musicians and the Metabolic Junk Boyz were born. They practised long and hard, an endeavour that has rendered me and I imagine, most of my peers immune to the charms of Bob Marley and America for all time.

The Boyz duly entered the competition, held in some grandeur and expectation at the Students' Union, with meandering renditions of 'Knocking on Heaven's Door' and

'Horse with No Name' in front of a large and largely bemused audience. They came last.

Chapter Fourteen

SWEETNESS AND LIGHT

There is nothing worse than people asking you what your favourite type of music is. It is the sort of party small talk that is guaranteed to either make my mind go immediately blank or for it to go into overdrive with possibilities and for me to blather on in complete embarrassment about stuff that I really don't like at all in an incoherent, endless diatribe. To your common or garden obsessive, the difficulties associated with this innocent question are enormous and giving a simple answer is nigh on impossible. For one thing, the emphasis of my favourite music changes in the short term, almost from day to day as genres come to the surface and then recede to make way for something else. Also, there are so many areas that I like, I can't think of them all at once. It is almost easier to say what it is that I don't like but then you just come across as very negative and depressive.

There is also a question of time. The music I liked when I was a student is not necessarily the music I like now, or liked when I was a child for that matter. The dilemma that presents itself boils down to whether you just take the plunge and go on and on about the intricacies of mid sixties Stax records or seventies glam and risk boring everyone to death, or whether you just keep everything on a lighter note and admit to liking Genesis and Fleetwood Mac in which case, if your inquisitor has been tipped off that you are 'a bit of a music buff', you risk making yourself look a complete fraud. The reality is that most of the time, people are not really interested but have asked to be polite and are therefore aghast to realise that you intend to give them an earnest and longwinded reply.

A close relation to the favourite music question is the question about your favourite band. All the same problems arise again. Do you talk about current favourites or past dalliances? Then there is the difficulty that I have a favourite for each type of music, be it rock, punk, soul, or whatever and they are all valid but that is not what people want to hear. It is almost impossible to pin down a favourite anything when you are a student of the subject but in order to avoid future awkwardness, I decided that I would have to try and formulate a proper answer, one that I could trot out at the appropriate moment. Having furnished myself with huge lists of artists and bands, I sat down to try and pick one upon which to base an answer. After a frustratingly long time, no answer had emerged, so it was only then that a more scientific method suggested itself.

Having learned the basics of musical theory, bought one or two records in my time and had some small exposure to the classical side of music, I felt that, armed with a blank sheet of paper, I should be able to formulate a discrete set of parameters that would specify my all-time favourite band. After much scribbling and extensive use of an eraser, it eventually looked like this:

Wanted – Favourite band. Must have:

a) A female singer of character
b) A male band of energy and invention
c) A band configuration based on either the guitar or else a completely unorthodox instrumental selection
d) A willingness to experiment with rhythm and dissonance
e) A twin towers writing team
f) An understanding in the use of the semitone in melody writing to imply key modulation
g) An ability to arrange vocals into interesting harmony

Having completed this exercise, I started to compare the bands I liked against this rather daunting specification. In fact, there turned out to be a whole stack of likely candidates, but in reality, few that came close to meeting all the requirements. Included in a list that ran to almost 50 bands were The Bangles, Blondie, Altered Images, Echobelly, Elastica, Ghost Dance, The Sundays and Penetration and whilst they all ticked a few of the boxes, none of them really came close to graduating to the final consideration list. More promising were Garbage, St Etienne and The Passions, all three of which I had liked for some time. Garbage I reluctantly dismissed for lacking in the vocal harmony department and St Etienne are perhaps a little too conventional. The Passions I liked a lot, particularly their single 'I'm in Love with a German Film Star' and the album '30,000 Feet Over China' which would still grace my list of favourite singles and albums respectively, but even they failed to convince on a number of counts. Recently I have had a close look at Evanescence but find their singer a little bland tonally and the music lacking in key areas.

After a long period of whittling, my final list contained just three names. The first was obviously Curved Air who fitted all seven counts, although if there was a weakness it was, again, in the vocal harmony section. Otherwise they were strong contenders. The second was Siouxsie and the Banshees whom I had followed for many years. They also fitted most of the requirements, having a unique, spartan sound capped by Siouxsie's Ice Maiden vocals but also fell down on the harmony point and do not really have a defined Twin Towers writing team.

It feels like I have spent most of my working life defending my fondness for Siouxsie and the Banshees as they were always seen by the majority as somehow threatening, rebellious and not really suitable for a man of my age to follow, largely due to Siouxsie's archetypal gothic image. Image is a strange attribute in that one particular image will stick in the mind despite having only a fleeting existence, whereas others never seem to register. Certainly the classic gothic image of Siouxsie Sioux with spiked hair and dog collars only lasted about two years around the time of the albums 'Ju Ju' and 'A Kiss in the Dreamhouse' between 1981 and 1982, despite having an enduring career that lasted more in the region of twenty years from the late 1970s to the late 1990s. Her image both before and after this short two-year period was significantly different, yet few remember this. I attended their gig in a circus tent in London's Finsbury Park in 1987 when, taking to the stage with her usual mop of black hair, Siouxsie suddenly whipped off what was revealed as a wig to expose her new neat, extremely short hair style and most of the female contingent in the audience dressed up as Siouxsie look-alikes, visibly wilted. So much for image. Nevertheless, I am gratified to note that although she has now retired to live in the French countryside, she still retains a little of that left field style that most of us remember her for and remains a true original.

Nevertheless, going back to my requirements list, both Curved Air and Siouxsie and the Banshees were strong contenders and in the 1970s and 1980s respectively there is no doubt that if asked, I would have had no doubts about giving them the accolade of favourite band, which underlines how the passage of time plays havoc with the answer to the question of favouritism. But I had to wait until 1989 to discover the real winner and the band that was the third on my final list.

And it was Lush. The trouble with citing Lush as my favourite band is that it tends to elicit the response, 'Who?' and justifiably so. Then I end up having to try and explain my choice. So here goes. Lush was a so-called indie band (recording for the independent record label; 4AD) who emerged out of the media labelled 'shoe-gazing' genre (a reference to several bands' propensity to look at their feet whilst playing) and comprised a bunch of hard partying liggers from Camden, London who specialised in a form of dreamy spaced-out pop, driven by layers of effects ridden guitars. Fronted by two female guitarist/singers; Emma Anderson and Miki Berenyi, who between them wrote all the material and backed up by a male rhythm section, Lush had a way with a melody or a chord progression that was positively inspired. I was particularly pleased to have discovered this band, as I immediately knew that they would tick all the boxes on my bands-you-will-like checklist. They contained the required Twin Towers writers in Miki and Emma, both of whom had a real grasp of the modulating melody, an enthusiastic, if flawed, female vocalist in Miki, a rhythm section in Steve Rippon on bass and Chris Acland on drums who were not averse to the odd Stravinsky-like primal beat and a knack of arranging choral harmonies around their melodies in a manner Mozart would have approved. Indeed, the ambience they managed to produce on their better material was strangely church-like. Lush were never hugely successful, but beavered away in Division Two trying harder to succeed than some of their peers in Division One, as often happens and I liked them a lot.

Stylistically, they looked an unusual combination on two counts. First was the purely cosmetic effect of Miki's Hungarian/Japanese parentage and red dyed hair juxtaposed to Emma's conventional dark English looks and the second was the gender division between the female guitarists and the male rhythm section. There was an unspoken tension between the girls' world-weary and marginally man-hating lyrics and the fact that the male half of the band was a necessity to realise their sentiments that gave the band a dangerously unstable ambience.

Miki's writing style is extrovert, instinctive and on occasion, deeply confessional. Her songs tend to rampage along with biting lyrics to the fore, but she also has a skill of layering melodies so that they form clever harmonies with each other. 'Kiss Chase' is a good example of the use of two melodies which when sung together form a chordal harmony of their own. She also has a slightly quirky quality that expresses itself in the use of unusual instruments, such as the recorder and her wry take on the eternal man-woman relationship. Generally in Twin Towers bands, the second writer has a very different style, but in this case, Emma's style is similar but more studied and introverted, with a bent towards atmospheric dance music, past and present. She also has an ear for creating huge aural soundscapes, which she then peppers with tunes in the style of the great melodies of the 1960s, whose mood she manages to invoke in a more contemporary setting. One of her more recent songs, 'Feels Like Summer' is a nod towards the Tamla Motown productions of Holland, Dozier and Holland with its heavily accented off beats and loose uplifting melody. Each of them seem equally at home writing up tempo rockers and reflective ballads.

Their career arc started in accordance with the Twin Towers plan with a sharp, edgy six track Mini album, 'Scar' containing some collaborative and some individual songs that have a unified band sound. I can't actually remember how I came to know about Lush or to be in possession of this CD, but I'm guessing it must have been reviewed in the NME and my sixth sense had picked it out. Anyhow, one day I arrived home with it and was bowled over. It was everything I had been looking for and a bit more. Every one of the songs boasted a suitably strange melody over an unconventional and energetic rhythm. The vocal harmonies, all delivered at the top end of the girls' singing range, were rich and occasionally discordant and the whole effect was stark and beautiful. In particular is a song called 'Thoughtforms' that is driven by its use of semitonal intervals that pushes the underlying harmony into all sorts of uncharted waters with great effect. You could almost see Bach nodding approvingly as it played.

Two more singles arrived and it became evident that not only were they an innovative band but that they gave unprecedented value for money. Each CD single contained no less than four songs, all of listenable quality, even when they were album rejects. The third single, 'Sweetness and Light' is one of my favourite examples of their early period dreamy hypnotic pop style and it raised expectations for the debut album.

Finally, after nearly four years, 'Spooky', their first album was released in 1992. Produced by Robin Guthrie of the Cocteau Twins, it had a dense swirling consistency that tended to engulf the band and take on a life of its own. This was mildly disappointing and Guthrie was roundly criticised for his production, which many felt, had not represented the band correctly, but had submerged the vocals in a mess of overproduced guitars. Unfortunately, having a musical partner, Elizabeth Fraser, who professes to sing lyrics in her own made up language was probably not going to help his defence. Nevertheless, the band's song-writing potential was realised for the most part and there were some engaging tracks like Miki's 'For Love' that promised well for the future.

Still following the plan, the really good stuff arrived with the release of Split, their second album. By this time Steve Rippon had left the band to be replaced on bass by Phil King. Also, Robin Guthrie had moved on and Mike Hedges whose producing credits include U2, Travis, Texas, Manic Street Preachers and The Cure, co-produced with the band. The result was an intoxicating concoction of chiming guitars, densely arranged rhythms and modulating melodies capped with those high-pitched girlish harmonies. If anything the album is a little too long in the way that CDs tend to be but this is nitpicking and it did include the venom-spitting single, 'Hypocrite', one of their finest songs. The album was a creative high point for Lush but although it was a critical success, it was not a commercial one, much to my disappointment (and theirs, probably).

Two years later, 'Lovelife' appeared and this turned out to be a completely different kettle of notes. Against the backdrop of the then prevalent Britpop sound, the album had a lighter, more pop orientated tone and in accordance with the Twin Towers plan, the two writers were now showing more individuality. As such the album didn't have quite the cohesive nature of 'Split'. There was more variety in the writing, highlighting the two distinct styles of the writers.

One track, 'Ciao!' involved Jarvis Cocker of Pulp in a light-hearted duet with Miki, while elsewhere, 'Last Night' revealed a heavy dance groove. Gone too, were the girls' high-pitched vocals and in their place were tunes sung in their mid to lower registers. Nevertheless, the album spawned no less than three hit singles in '500 (Shake Baby Shake)', 'Ladykillers' featuring Miki's new low register growl and one of the most perfect two-and-a-half minute pop singles ever, 'Single Girl'.

Penned by Emma, this is the sort of single you would play to a visiting alien from Gamma-delta 5, to explain what all the fuss is about when the conversation turned to popular music. It has everything: a racy introduction, the catchiest of catchy ABC tunes, a rumbustuous guitar-driven rhythm, a false ending, a rhythm change in the middle section, a guitar solo and finally, a killer coda taking you out to the fade. All this contained within a two minute and thirty-five second shell. Frankly, you are unlikely to hear a better constructed song in two-and-a-bit minutes unless you go back through the Beatles' early catalogue. Most singles these days are at least three or even four minutes long without half the variety of this single and suffer accordingly. Ever noticed how music shows on television often foreshorten them? As a consequence of all this heady success, Lush appeared on Top of the Pops twice, one appearance introduced with some irony by competitor at the time Louise Wener of the band Sleeper.

It seemed that Lush was teetering on the verge of the big time but then, after 'Lovelife' came disaster: in 1996 their drummer, Chris Acland committed suicide. The band went silent for sometime and then announced that they were not continuing. I was shattered, probably for the first time since I was a teenager mourning the loss of Curved Air. In a way it's comforting to know that music can still affect a hardened cynic like me, but as a forty something I really didn't think that it ever would again. But I grieved for Lush in a way that would have befitted a Take That or a Bay City Rollers fan but with more of a stiff upper lip. I now take comfort from the fact that I own a fine body of work that no amount of subsequent, poorer work can tarnish. It was inevitable that, as a Twin Towers band, one or both of the writers would eventually leave so all that unpleasantness has been avoided and my memories of them remain fondly nostalgic.

Following the split, Miki Berenyi disappeared, Phil King joined the Jesus and Mary Chain and Emma Anderson is now to be found writing songs and playing guitar with vocalist Lisa O'Neill under the name Sing-Sing and very good they are too. Emma's song-writing has matured under the expanded musical remit of Sing-Sing and her complex melody driven songs are still a joy to behold.

In the aftermath of their demise the knowledge that still eats away at me was that I never saw them play live, yet I had two opportunities to do so. The first came in their early years around 1989 when I actually had a ticket to see them in my possession but when the great day arrived, I was too ill to attend. I still have the unused ticket to remind me. The second opportunity arose just before they split in 1996. They were due to play a short set at the Virgin Megastore in Oxford Street, London to promote 'Lovelife' during a weekday lunch hour. Fate can be unbelievably cruel and that day she pulled out all the stops. The Virgin store is a few hundred yards from the office where I worked, but that day one of our clients decided to do a large deal and we were on standby as advisers, should we be needed. That meant no going out of the office at lunchtime in case of being called to attend meetings or undertake some urgent task. We waited and waited as the minutes ticked by in an agony of anticipation. Just one phone call to let us off the hook would be enough to see me scuttle down Oxford Street – but none came. The appointed time for their appearance came and went and we heard nothing and I had missed them, unknowingly, for the last time. Soon afterwards they were no more and my chance had gone.

A final thought. It never ceases to amaze me how musical styles can turn up in the most unusual surroundings. Laying their haunting melodies over swathes of dense guitar and surging rhythms, Lush always sounded far too noisy and anarchic to have a sense of classical choral harmony as represented by say, Handel's Messiah. Yet strip away the façade and what was left were a bunch of songs that were carried by some exquisite harmony work. Tucked away on one of their final single releases, 'Ladykillers' is a track called 'Dear Me'. This is a demonstration recording of a song by Miki Berenyi made at home by Miki herself on an 8-track recorder and it is one of the most interesting things I have ever heard her attempt. It comprises a collage of vocal lines that lilts along in 3/4 (waltz) time over a very sparse backing forming a circular melody that loops over and over as more and more vocal harmonies are added. Then, to add drama, a second melodic loop is added to the mix that also gains harmonies as it goes until the whole thing spirals ever upwards to a cacophonous climax. It is quite stunning and I am at a loss as to why this was never converted to a full band number. Perhaps the rest of them didn't like it, but Handel would've loved it.

Like one bereaved, I have never had the heart to get involved with any other band to date so, for the moment, Lush will continue to be my favourite band of all time and will be cited as such when the next unsuspecting person asks me.

Chapter Fifteen

REVOLUTION 9

For a long period of my academic career during the years of 1975–1976, I felt dislocated from the music industry and accordingly, bought next to nothing new in the way of records and for two good reasons. There was nothing worth buying and I was skint. Progrock was dead, Glam was dominant, 'Hotel California' was top of the Capital Hitline for weeks on end and corporate rock ruled.

It was for this reason and the fact that I had heard their version of 'Light My Fire' on the radio that I became interested in the late 1960s music of the Doors again. As you will remember, I had tried this avenue once before and just couldn't get to like them. But during my wasteland years at university, I decided to give them another chance and disposed of precious funds in purchase of the double compilation album 'Weird Scenes Inside the Goldmine'. Somehow, this time around we got along a lot better and inspired again, I became a firm fan. There is no doubt that the Doors' eerie foretelling of the Stranglers' sound was all that kept me sane during those dark times. Luckily, salvation was just around the corner, albeit with a safety pin through its nose.

All things come to those who wait, or so I've been informed and it was towards the end of my time at University that the rallying call of the punk revolution was to be heard on the horizon. At last there was something new and vibrant to listen to and visions of exhilarating concerts at the students' union began to materialise. It was when I started buying singles by the Sex Pistols, Generation X and the Adverts that my satisfaction with life improved no end but at the same time things became a little fraught socially. Whilst my circle of fellow students were quite happy to be aligned with Steeleye Span, Steely Dan and the Eagles, eyebrows were raised at my new collection of singles and the reception awaiting my copy of 'Rattus Norvegicus' by the Stranglers was more than a little frosty. It is all too clear now that these were the first signs that my life would not follow the same course as most others and that a degree of secrecy would be needed if I were to remain socially acceptable.

During my second year, I had taken up with a first year food science undergraduate, Julie. Looking back, it seems almost inevitable that I would gravitate to her as a previous boyfriend of hers was Gary Lagan, a record producer who would go on to form ZTT records with Paul Morley and Trevor Horn. Luckily, despite owning records by Cat Stevens and Donovan and having to have her copy of Peter Frampton's infamous 'Frampton Comes Alive!' double live album surgically removed from her grasp, she was all in favour of the new wave, so the going wasn't all uphill but there was no doubt that a social marker had been positioned and it would only be a few years before it was claimed. She was also a great Nilsson fan and would play his histrionic version of Badfinger's 'Without You' regularly. You see, one great cover is worth a thousand poorly conceived ones.

Julie had a younger brother, Jerry, who I first met when he was just fifteen, but with whom I would remain friends long after Julie and I had parted and she was settled with a husband and children. Although we had chatted about musical subjects on our several meetings, the defining moment occurred during Julie's 21st birthday party at her parents' house in Surrey. Jerry and I had teamed up to look after the music and about half way through the evening during which time we had stuck firmly to the sort of party music that everyone finds non threatening, I had produced a 7 inch copy of the Stranglers' 'No More Heroes' (with picture sleeve, naturally) and with some trepidation, suggested that we play it.

'OK,' he said nonchalantly.

'OK?' I thought.

Not 'You must be joking!'

Or 'Not bloody likely!'

After the period of sustained aggravation I had received from my university friends concerning my choice of punk music, this was a totally unexpected reaction and a not unwelcome one. We played it, nobody fainted or contacted the police and we became musical allies from about that point forwards.

At the end of the interminably hot summer of 1976 and with the university exams completed, Julie, Jerry and I attended Queen's free concert in Hyde Park. I have never been a great fan of outdoor events of this nature, as the long hours of boredom in the heat of the day defending a few square feet of ground against thousands of others whilst the support acts play is never really outweighed by the eventual arrival of the headliners. Admittedly, my experience of all-day outdoor events is limited to this one and my attendance at Knebworth in 1975 when the Pink Floyd unveiled their follow up to 'Dark Side of the Moon', the worthy 'Wish You Were Here' and played both of them in their entirety, live. On both occasions a good spot was obtained within half a mile of the stage only to find ourselves at the back of the surging crowd with little or no view, when the main act started. Most outdoor venues have no natural slope of sufficient incline to allow everybody a view of the stage and unless you are a good six inches taller than the national average, there is little hope of an unrestricted view. To compound the sense of exclusion is the synchronicity factor. As a consequence of the relatively slow speed of sound compared to that of light, anyone standing about two hundred yards from the stage hears the sound of what they are seeing some half a second later. Whilst this doesn't sound much it is more than enough to dislocate the sound and pictures entering your brain so that it begins to resemble a poorly made film where the audio soundtrack is not matched to the video accurately.

On this occasion the support acts included Rufus, Steve Hillage and Kiki Dee, fresh from her chart-topping duet with Elton John on 'Don't Go Breaking My Heart'. I am ashamed to admit that I have absolutely no recollection of Rufus, despite being fronted by an emerging Chaka Khan, but I can remember that Steve Hillage was reasonably diverting, if you enjoy spaced-out psychedelic guitar and bobble hats. I must have been reasonably impressed with his performance (and potential for nomination in the Barking Mad category, bobble hat division) as I bought his 'L' album soon after, but not so taken with it that it didn't find its way onto a sales list some years later in one of my ill advised clearouts.

Of the remainder, Kiki Dee was better than may have been expected and on the night, Queen sounded great but were little more than dots on the horizon after the statutory crowd surge and with the heat and sense of claustrophobia, we were left wondering whether it was all worthwhile. These days I'd probably watch it on television from the comfort of my sofa.

Jerry and I also had a common interest in early Genesis records, which would be analysed to death over the obligatory beer. I have always been a 'Gabriel and Hackett' man when it comes to Genesis, preferring their albums from their progressive period of 1971 to 1976 when they were a five piece of some talent and invention. I always considered their work musically challenging, occasionally wryly humorous and containing a modicum of smile-inducing English eccentricity. Once the band had been reduced to three, I sensed that their output had lost the variety and sensitivity that Steve Hackett's guitar brought them and the individual lyrics and general weirdness that Peter Gabriel contributed. Their 1978 effort after both Peter and Steve had left, 'And Then There Were Three' was endlessly debated with Jerry and his school friend, Ashley, but we couldn't really find anything to embrace. I continued to buy their albums up to 'Abacab' but found it hard going, especially in the face of the vigour of the new wave. 'Abacab' can now be found in my Worst Albums of all Time list. As Sod's Law would have it and having made the decision to stop buying Genesis records, their next album contained the encouragingly good 'Mama' but I wasn't to be tempted back.

But it was Fil, the boyfriend of Julie's friend, Rachel, who introduced me to Steve Hackett, the solo artist. Fil resided in one of the residential halls on the far side of the campus and had a penchant for wearing hats, which clearly made him an authority on matters musical. At the same time as Genesis' 'A Trick of the Tail' was released in 1976, he lent me Steve Hackett's debut solo album, 'Voyage of the Acolyte' so that for a time, I had both albums to compare. This was the moment when, much to my surprise, I became a Hackett fan as I found that his own work was more interesting than Genesis, despite the acknowledged quality of 'A Trick of the Tail'. Hackett's style is that of the true guitarist, equally at home with classical acoustic and the rock electric versions of the instrument and his music embodies both styles. His playing always evokes a certain sentimentality that lends a marginally melancholic air to any piece he is involved with. Although not averse to the macho leanings of guitar soloing, his resultant style is slightly more feminine in texture that was ideally suited to Genesis' early, more pastoral works. A good example of his atmospheric style is the middle section of 'The Knife' from the 1973 'Live' album where his technique of starting a note from the top of a bend (where a string is pulled to shorten it thus producing a higher note), and then letting the note fall gives a yearning quality to his playing. I thought that his 'Voyage of the Acolyte' was instrumentally inventive with that slight melancholic air about the themes that was somehow old, almost medieval, and mystical, especially 'Shadow of the Hierophant' hauntingly sung by Sally Oldfield, Mike's sister.

I bought all his solo output during the late 1970s and into the early 1980s but let it drop when the quality started to wane. I always felt that Steve was more of a team player and that his best contributions involved adding to and embellishing other's work, hence his invaluable contribution to Genesis, a contribution they sorely missed. On his own, the material started to take on a samey quality. However, I picked up on his career later in the 1980s when he released a series of albums such as 'Momentum' containing only solo acoustic guitar pieces. These were real gems, extending the promise showed in pieces like 'Horizons' from Genesis' 'Foxtrot' some fifteen years before. The writing varied from pure classical styles to more blues and folk pieces and all of them were expertly played. As a guitarist still trying to master this style, I was greatly envious.

Whilst all this critical discussion was fine as far as it went, it wasn't much help on the live music front. But true to the nature of the time, my university banned all punk bands from playing live at the union, so by the end of my student tenure there was little to see in the way of new bands and I left in the summer of 1977 without too much regret.

Jerry and I started to frequent concerts further afield and the late 1970s were a prime time for live bands. In quick succession, we saw Blondie, XTC, Talking Heads, Siouxsie and the Banshees, The Cure and The Stranglers. At most of these events we mingled with the bin liners, dog collars and spiked hair looking like two refugees from Marks and Spencer, but then as Jerry would say, 'In this environment, who is the more radical?'

This was a golden age for live shows where the best of the new wave was displayed with invention and vitality. My only disappointing memory is attached to that most oddball of bands: The Monochrome Set. I had purchased their 1980 album, 'Strange Boutique' after hearing a track or two on the radio and had taken to its English eccentricity and great tunes immediately. So much so, that I jumped at the chance to see them live at the YMCA in Tottenham Court Road, London. I'd never entered this imposing concrete block prior to this event and as it turned out, the venue was a little disconcerting, being about three miles underground down a spiral staircase. Once at the bottom, an underground cavern opened out and in due course, the Set turned up to play. But something wasn't right and I didn't know whether it was down to them or me. It was one of those occasions where I found no connection with the band and after about half the set I went outside under a cloud of despair only to find several others milling around with the same view. We chatted for a bit whilst the band laboured below and eventually, I went home in a philosophical frame of mind to live another day. There are always times like these but it is difficult to understand what goes wrong. On occasion, it is the misrepresentation that a single album confers that becomes apparent during a live set when the true character of the band emerges but whether this was the case here I shall never know; I never bought any other of their albums to find out.

By the mid 1980s, I was living in a small one bedroomed flat in a newly constructed, purpose built block in Ealing, whilst Jerry had moved southwards from his parents' house to a place in Redhill, near Reigate. The journey by car from Ealing to Redhill across Greater London is one of the most tortuous known to man and involves a route that includes negotiation of the north circular road, Chiswick roundabout, Kew Bridge, the south circular, the A306, the A3 as far as Tolworth, the A240 and finally the A217 across the M25 and into Redhill. I used to do this journey regularly on weekday evenings to meet up and socialise but after a while it began to play on my nerves. From Ealing to Redhill during the late rush hour was usually at least an hour's journey, but coming home later that evening, the time could usually be cut to around 40–45 minutes. In fact, about the length of a long vinyl album.

It dawned on me that this was the answer to the sheer boredom of the journey. Soon, a game was developed whereby I would pick an album (taped for use in the car) start it up in Redhill and try to get home before the album finished. Many albums at that time ran for barely 35 minutes which was far too short if you intended to keep your driving licence but the one I found to be a real tester was Belinda Carlisle's first solo effort, 'Heaven On Earth' which clocked in at 43 minutes and 26 seconds. This time limit was achievable without breaking all the speed limits, but would not be tolerant of traffic queues and hold-ups. After several attempts at this time, certain landmarks became important pointers. At the end of side one and the beginning of side two there is a run of three gorgeous songs, one by Belinda's ex-Go Gos bandmate, Charlotte Caffey and two by the ubiquitous Diane Warren. These acted as an accurate gauge to progress as they would play out as I hared up the A3 trunk road in the outside lane but if I had not reached the Robin Hood roundabout by the time 'I Get Weak' had finished, I would be lucky to beat the clock that evening. The second marker, if time was becoming tight, would be coming over Kew Bridge to the up tempo 'Nobody Owns Me' and tearing up the north circular to Ealing common when the final track, 'Love Never Dies' started. Luckily this last song ran to over five minutes so even if it appeared to be running towards the end by the time I turned into the Uxbridge Road, there was probably just enough left to reach my flat.

As with all obsessives, we all had a dream, however unlikely, of stardom. All of us in our little circle of friends had toyed with being musicians and we all had managed to learn to play a few guitar chords but by the late 1980s, Jerry's friend, Ashley had taught himself bass guitar to a standard well beyond the rest of us and with two school friends, Mick and his brother, Paddy, had formed a three piece band calling themselves 'A Thousand Islands'. Mick, the singer and guitarist wrote most of the material and they settled comfortably into that 1980s funk pop sound exemplified by bands like Level 42 and Orange Juice. The rest of us, as friends of the band, did the necessary support act by attending their live gigs in seedy pubs and, on one occasion, the dizzy heights of the Ashley Centre in Epsom. They even produced a cassette album of nine songs, complete with photocopied cover depicting the three of them arranged around various coils of rope in a vaguely nautical way.

Having watched a few of those band history programmes that turn up on television from time to time, I have always been struck by how cut-throat the whole band business is. The life of a rock band is evidently a cauldron of naked ambition, bruised egos and the clash of artistic temperaments. Most of the bands featured in these programmes always seem to fall prey to sackings, leavings and fallings out in a big way. Not to mention the violence, the years on non-speaking terms and the broken love affairs. Members leave and rejoin only to leave again with alarming frequency. It seems that the world of the music industry is as ruthless as the Capitalism it is based upon is always made out to be, despite indications that most musicians are determinately leftwards leaning, politically. Sadly, the story of A Thousand Islands turned out to be no different.

Fuelled by an ambition to break into the big time, A Thousand Islands hired a manager and sought to play before record company A&R representatives at every opportunity. To help in this quest, it was decided that what the band needed was a specialist singer – someone who was a charismatic front man and someone who could take the weight off Mick's shoulders and let him concentrate on writing and playing guitar. After a while a candidate emerged and his name was Mike Christer. Not only was Mike a strong singer, he could play a mean guitar and could write as well. His multi talents seemed a major asset to the band and as a newly formed four piece, A Thousand Islands hit the audition trail with gusto. Whilst the addition of Christer was seen as a good thing, it became apparent that his own material was increasingly ousting their stock of songs and that he was taking over lead guitar chores, relegating Mick to rhythm playing. In short, Christer was slowly taking over the band from the inside. Whilst there was a small degree of unease over the way events were unfolding, everyone suppressed these feelings for the good of the band. The tensions were building, but there was worse to come.

To everyone's sincere delight, they eventually impressed the right person enough to land a deal with Virgin Records for three albums. It seemed too good to be true and the problem was that it was. The cracks finally appeared when the band turned up at the recording studio to start work on their debut album. The producer assigned to their case immediately took exception to Mick's guitar work and Paddy's drumming, claiming that neither was up to scratch. He wanted them out of the band and was unmoveable. His stance immediately tipped the band into conflict, a conflict that their manager seemed unwilling to resolve. It also placed Ashley, as the only original band member not to be given his marching orders, in an impossible position. His unenviable choice was either to fulfil his dream and stick with Christer whilst alienating himself from his long time friends or give up the opportunity and leave the band in a show of solidarity. After a period of agonising indecision, he agreed to stick with it on the basis that this was a once in a lifetime opportunity.

The recording of the album was moved to New York and Ashley and Mike Christer, now under the working band name of 'Still Life' duly flew to the USA to record the album, comprising all Christer songs, with session players filling in the missing instruments. The album, titled 'A Definite Maybe' appeared on Virgin records in 1991, under the name 'Christer' ostensibly making it a Mike Christer solo album with Ashley credited as one of the musicians. Three singles, complete with videos brimming with attractive models, were released from the album and the band toured the UK as support act for a momentarily rejuvenated Orchestral Manoeuvres in the Dark, but no real public interest was shown despite the sterling efforts of 'Whispering' Bob Harris on his night-time radio show, who championed the album. Virgin showed no committed signs of wanting to promote the band as they were having financial difficulties of their own which eventually resulted in a takeover. Meanwhile, the album was left to flounder and Christer was quietly dropped by Virgin in a roster clearout some time after. Ashley went back to his day job and eventually rebuilt bridges with his erstwhile band mates and the rock dream faded forever.

This is the nearest I have ever come to actually knowing anyone famous in the music industry, as opposed to knowing someone who knows someone famous. My brother, after years of trying for a recording deal with various bands – Moonstone, Vagrant and latterly, Hardware – has never had any luck and Ashley's experience was a sobering realisation of the way the music industry can consume and then spit out its prodigies.

Chapter Sixteen

WE ARE FAMILY

Families, eh? Who needs them? Well, quite a few bands, that's for sure. It really is quite staggering to realise how many brothers, sisters and cousins there are lurking in the world of popular music. In a brief survey of my own collection of records and CDs, I counted no less than 18 instances of family members in bands and that, you may be gratified to know, does not include anything by the Nolans, Osmonds, Jacksons, Bros, Hanson or Five Star, but does include obvious candidates like the Pointer Sisters and the Corrs. Scarcely believable, I know, but there they all are, these brothers and sisters, from Sparks (Ron & Russell Mael) to The Kinks (Ray & Dave Davies), from the Bangles (Vicki & Debbie Peterson) to Martha and the Muffins (Tim & Mark Gane) and onwards through the Undertones (John & Damian O'Neill) and Oasis (Noel & Liam Gallagher) to the Darkness (Justin & Dan Hawkins). It seems that the rock world just can't do without them and this contention is all the more apparent now that the ultimate family band has arrived in the form of the Magic Numbers who comprise no less than two brother/sister pairings in Romeo and Michele Stodart and Sean and Angela Gannon. They will be hard to beat.

The obvious advantage that is immediately apparent from the act of forming a band from your own family is that they are always available for rehearsals with little excuse, especially if you all live in the same house. Equally obvious is that it negates the need to stick grubby pieces of paper in the local record shop saying, 'Drummer required. Must be into Hendrix etc' and even worse, paying out real money to advertise in the various music papers. I have never had to do this myself but I imagine that advertising for band members is a precarious business as you never know who will turn up and more worryingly, you never know whether you can get rid of them again. The experience of heavy metal band Black Sabbath always haunts me in this respect. The story goes, by all accounts, that the guitarist, drummer and bassist had already got together and were looking for a singer. They had advertised in the local press, but only one reply had been received, from someone signing himself, mysteriously, as 'Ozzy'. Now read on (in a broad Brummie accent):

First band member: 'What have you done about it?'

Second band member: 'I've asked him to come round here at eight, tonight.'

First band member: 'OK. I used to know an Ozzy at school, you know. Mental he was. Hope it isn't him!'

Sound effect: Door bell rings.

Newcomer: 'Hello, I'm Ozzy'

All: 'Aaaaarrrgghh!'

No wonder giving your brother or sister a try out seems such a good idea at the time.

Actually, I should know because I did it myself. I had and indeed still have a younger brother, Dave, who at the time of my guitar purchase was eager to have a go himself. So, in order to have a bit of fun playing with other people and avoiding all that messy business about having to find others and then getting on with them socially, I taught him the rudiments of guitar playing, just as I had taught myself. After a decent interval where he went away and practised, this worked a treat and we had some fun times jamming around songs we knew. However, the full realisation of what I had done was not long in coming. The next thing I knew he had attained a level of competence that was far above mine and what was worse, he had formed a band with some friends of his and was playing gigs at the local pubs and supporting named bands. This was the beginning of a long but low-key career playing in various bands at pub and small hall level without getting a break into the big time. His one moment of glory came in 1981 and involved an appearance on Top of the Pops acting as part of a backing band for Keith Marshall, whom you probably won't remember, performing his solitary hit 'Only Crying'. Whilst this caused not a little excitement in the Warminger household, it caused even more at the Inland Revenue, who then pursued him relentlessly for years afterwards, under the mistaken belief that he was a real rock star.

Not just content with playing in a band, Dave also had the outrageous good fortune to be in the same class at secondary school with Argent bassist Jim Rodford's son, Steven. This was all too much, but it didn't stop me engineering an opportunity of getting to meet him to talk music. This elicited an invitation to his parents' house, close to ours in St Albans to record one of my songs on his personal reel-to-reel recorder. At the time, I only had a handful to choose from and so selected one of my very early songs with the stolen poem lyrics but luckily he didn't seem to notice the rather exotic words and seemed genuinely interested in recording it. The reason for this became apparent once we were ensconced in his music room – he had a full drum kit set up *and* he could play it. Much to my horror, as I was the only one who knew the song, I was to sing the lyrics as well as play guitar. My brother would handle bass and Steven would drum and act as recording engineer. The first task was for me to teach the others the song and was mildly impressed with the speed at which the others picked it up. Then, with the aid of borrowed guitars, the three of us played much of the backing track together directly onto tape and after numerous takes, managed to get something resembling music in the can, as we music types say.

Unfortunately the big moment had then arrived: it was my turn to sing. Steven produced a large tea chest, which had been padded inside to act as a sort of anechoic chamber, designed to remove all surplus echo and I was supposed to stick my head in it with a microphone and sing. It was claustrophobic and dark inside the box but with gallons of adrenaline coursing through my veins, I did my utmost and hoped for the best. The recording process requires that the singer wear headphones so that the already recorded backing track can be played as a vocal guide. This makes singing quite difficult, as you cannot hear yourself properly. In later years, I learnt to remove one earpiece in order to hear my own voice but at this point I was a recording novice. In the circumstances I thought I had done a reasonable job but on pulling my head out of the box I found the other two rolling around the floor in hysterics. I was that good. Once they had recovered, I pressed my case that the box had to go. Unfortunately my winning the argument saw me sitting on the stairs outside the room doing the vocal track. Quite what the Rodfords thought of this disembodied voice drifting into their living room is anybody's guess but many takes and several hours of recording and mixing the results later, the reel of tape containing the completed song was held in our sticky hands.

I still have a very poor cassette copy of this endeavour and what it shows plainly, from a distance of thirty odd years, is some extremely competent drumming from a teenaged Steven, some dreadful guitar work from the Warminger brothers and vocals that should be erased if only I could separate them from the rest of the mix. But none of that mattered at the time as the heady exhilaration of creation had taken over and for a few delirious hours we were pop stars. The song wasn't that bad either and with Steven's assured drumming pushing it along, it sounded better than I could have hoped and certainly better than me playing it alone on a single acoustic guitar. I could feel a yearning growing inside me to write and record my own songs – but how?

Just to add a measure of perspective to this achievement, at the time of writing, Steven Rodford is playing drums with Rod Argent and Colin Blunstone in the reformed Zombies, my brother Dave is playing bass as a member of a Hertfordshire based band called Hardware and I have tactfully retired from recording and am writing this.

So on the subject of younger brothers, I sympathise with Tim Finn entirely. There you are with a nifty if not wildly successful band called Split Enz and what do you do? In your own magnanimous way, you airily invite your younger brother, Neil, to play guitar and the next thing you know, he's written your only top twenty hit, 'I Got You' and has then left to form some band called Crowded House and has a raft of mega hits including 'Don't Dream Its Over', 'Four Seasons in One Day' and 'Weather With You'. There is something incredibly infuriating about younger brothers and sometimes you just feel like laying one on him. And if you were Ray or Dave Davies or Noel or Liam Gallagher you probably would because brothers in bands have this in-built propensity to brawl, either on stage or off. This well documented male trait never seems to affect sisters. You can't imagine an on-stage fracas between, say, the Corr sisters or The Dixie Chicks. Yet there is clearly a fair amount of aggravation involved in setting up shop with your own family if the strike rate is anything to go by. Some just leave quietly like David Knopfler from Dire Straits whilst others like the Davies or Gallagher brothers hang around in a frenzy of sibling rivalry and create a degree of friction that keeps the Tabloids amused for years.

Another aspect of the family connections in rock phenomenon is the family as a business configuration as exemplified by the Wilde family. Marty Wilde was a great British singing star of the late 1950s and early 1960s with hits such as 'A Teenager in love' and 'Rubber Ball'. He married Joyce Baker of the Vernon Girls and they produced a son Ricki and a daughter Kim, who then had a string of hits in the 1980s from 'Kids in America' to 'Never Trust a Stranger' before her career tailed off in the 1990s. During that time, most of her material was written by brother Ricki with input from father Marty and she was managed by Marty, so keeping everything in house. I'd always had a soft spot for Kim Wilde, especially her early singles like the razor sharp 'View from a Bridge' and most of her late 1980s albums and was saddened when she gave it all up to be a TV gardener. In particular, there is a late album called 'Love Is' which I guess to be her 'Laura Ashley' period, judging by the CD cover. By this stage in her career, top American song writer Rick Nowells had been drafted in to produce and write some material along with Ricki Wilde and Kim herself and the album is full of amiable songs in a Belinda Carlislish sort of way (hardly surprising as Rick was writing for Belinda as well), but by this time the public had moved on as so often happens. A great shame, but our loss is gardening's gain.

The Wilde family also point to another phenomenon that has become noticeable since the 1980s and that is the rise of the second-generation star. Since rock 'n' roll is not that old, this has never happened until now but sons and daughters are now lining up to have a bash at stardom in the footsteps of their famous parents with somewhat mixed results. Along with Kim Wilde are Julian and Sean Lennon, Chesney Hawkes (son of Chip Hawkes of the Tremeloes), Alisha's Attic (daughters of Brian Poole, the original Tremeloes frontman), Wilson Phillips (daughters of Brian Wilson of the Beach Boys and John & Michelle Phillips of the Mamas and Papas), Eliza Carthy (daughter of folk legend, Martin Carthy) and Kelly Osbourne (daughter of Ozzy), who have all had a stab at chart success. Clearly this is only the beginning and as time rolls on and future generations rise to the surface, more will reveal themselves. But do second generation stars have any advantage as a result of their name? Certainly, Kim Wilde and the American Wilson Phillips have both enjoyed reasonable success, but poor Chesney will always be known amongst the one hit wonders, despite his luck in securing Nik Kershaw's mesmerisingly good song, 'The One and Only'. The sample is currently too small to draw any firm conclusions but based on the assumption that the majority of their audience will be too young to fully acknowledge their parentage it is safe to predict that most second-generation stars will be judged in the same way as everybody else. I doubt that Kim Wilde's success was built on the back of her father's, some twenty-five years before.

One other, slightly unsettling aspect of the generational phenomenon is that there now exists the possibility of bands being resurrected in the next generation like some gruesome cloning exercise. We could be subjected to The Beatles mark 2 comprising James McCartney, Julian or Sean Lennon and Dhani Harrison on guitars and Zak Starkey on drums. The most alarming facet of this is that all of them have the musical acumen to fulfil the needs of the experiment, but I sincerely hope that it never happens, for all our sakes.

The generational aspect of the music business can also be seen in a more beneficial light in the way certain of the established stars have a hand in the development of a new generation of artists. In this respect the industry as a whole can be loosely envisaged as a 'family'. Anyone interested in the early career of Kate Bush will know that, as a teenager, she was discovered and then initially mentored by the Pink Floyd's Dave Gilmour before releasing 'Wuthering Heights'. It is interesting to see how members of the older generation are now writing material for the newer stars, often in a style quite unlike that of their own career. Here I am thinking of Max Martin, a member of a Scandinavian heavy metal band prior to writing pure pop hits like 'Baby, One More Time' and 'Oops, I Did it Again' for Britney Spears and Phil Thornalley, an ex-member of The Cure, who co-wrote Natalie Imbruglia's perfect debut single 'Torn'. Come to think about it, the Australian soap invasion often appears to be fuelled by UK songwriters. Kylie Minogue's huge hit, 'Can't Get You Out of My Head' was written by Rob Davis of 1970s glam rock giants, Mud and Cathy Dennis, who had a run of top twenty singles herself in the early 1990s (and wrote 'Toxic' for Britney Spears). In all these cases, it is the mix of styles, akin to the Twin Towers effect, that is helping to synthesise new creations.

But the real advantage of family bands is in the voices. There is nothing quite like the blending of family voices to produce the most gorgeous of harmony singing and if you really need proof of this assertion, go and listen to anything by the Beach Boys or the Everly Brothers or even the Osmonds. The fact that family voices are hewn from the same genes and are therefore fundamentally the same yet have just enough individuality to separate them, is worth more than every studio double tracking device in existence. There is something otherworldly about the interlocking voices of the Everly Brothers on 'All I Have to do is Dream' or the Beach Boys during the final choral segment of 'Surf's Up' that almost defies description. There is a magical chemistry acting in many family centred bands from the Beach Boys (three brothers and a cousin), to Sister Sledge (er... sisters) and the Bee Gees (brothers) and it always produces the same kind of awe inspiring choral sound. In view of my love of choral works, I try to seek out sibling pairings in the hope that there will exist that synergy that only evolves in such situations. Failing that you could always take a chance on slightly more unusual combinations like American country duo, the Judds' mother and daughter pairing or even the Sinatra's father and daughter collaboration.

Which brings us inexorably to duets. My only question here is why? Why do artists and particularly well-known artists, have this irrepressible urge to sing duets with each other, apart from the obvious benefit of earning them pots of money on the back of their combined celebrity? The charts always have at least one of these abominations hanging around at any one time and each one is virtually without exception the sort of dog's dinner that any self-respecting dog would turn his nose up at. I've already alluded to the dreadful version of 'Dancing in the Street' by Messrs Jagger and Bowie, but the classic example that embodies everything that is wrong with big name duets is 'Ebony and Ivory', a collaboration from the early 1980s by Paul McCartney and Stevie Wonder. For starters, the song is only average and you might think that that is bad enough but that is not the real problem with this recording. It is that their voices are just not compatible and worse still, each mercilessly highlights the faults in the other. McCartney is a controlled, highly accurate vocalist whilst Wonder's voice is much looser and broader in interpretation and this combination leads to an uncomfortable clash of styles from which neither walks away unscathed. In the glare of McCartney's pure accuracy, Wonder sounds dreadfully undisciplined and off colour whilst Wonder's broad singing style makes McCartney sound stiff and stilted by comparison. This is the major drawback that engulfs most duet pairings and it is that they are just not vocally seamless, in the way that sibling vocalists are, or anyone else for that matter.

Worse still is the obvious cynicism apparent in the pairing of two singing stars who never even meet to record the song. They need not even like each other but are able to benefit financially from the resultant somewhat false liaison. Modern technology has allowed singers in different parts of the world to create duets without moving from their respective countries to do so. Perhaps I am being naïve here but if by some hideous twist of fate (for her) I was to record something with Madonna, you can be assured that I would want to meet her and record the vocals together in the same place at the same time. Is this too much to ask? The answer is obviously, yes, but I would still place duets in the same category as live albums and that is; avoid wherever possible.

As usual, there are always a few exceptions to every rule and in the case of duets, my favourite is 'Kids' by Robbie Williams and Kylie Minogue. You could probably hear the cash registers ringing all around the world when this idea was first mooted, but this one works brilliantly. To kick off, it has a rollicking good tune, which by itself would be enough to ensure success for either of them, but it also contains a magical harmony-laden chorus and best of all, two singers whose voices gel in a way that most others don't and it's not because they are spectacularly great singers because they're not. Although Robbie is an exulted holder of the Warminger

'Queen Test' Award, his is not a technically brilliant voice but an enthusiastic and characterful one. Similarly, Kylie has a bubbly yet average voice that is well suited to this type of disco meets rock material. But together, they sound perfect and if every other duet was created with this type of care, I wouldn't be moaning about them here.

Families in rock are a bit like families in real life, you can't live with them, but you can't live without them and in the case of Bros, nobody else wanted to live with them either, ask Craig Logan. In the arena of vocal harmony, they are untouched but you wouldn't want to go on a year long tour with them without a bodyguard.

Chapter Seventeen

WORKING IN A COALMINE

Putting his pen down on the desk, he shuffled in his seat and with a rueful grin, looked at me and said, 'You know, for a supposedly intelligent bloke, you don't half listen to some rubbish!'

What could I say? After all, I was new, he was a senior colleague and I didn't really want to make an issue of it, and there was always the possibility that he was right, so I just laughed it off and agreed. The conversation that had preceded this remark was all to do with the latest single from Swindon's finest, XTC and had taken place across the desks at my first place of employment. I had propounded the theory that 'Making Plans for Nigel' was possibly their best single to date and that Terry Chambers' inventive tom tom and hi-hat rhythm underpinning Andy Partridge's and Dave Gregory's syncopated guitar riffs was leagues above the standard so-called new wave fare of the day. Clearly, my colleague didn't agree, but this was not unusual and I was beginning to understand that talking popular music in the working environment was just not the done thing and was likely to single you out as untrustworthy and not really promotion material.

But I knew I was right – it was a great single. In 1992, about thirteen years after this conversation took place, the BBC dramatised Ruth Rendell's mystery novel *A Fatal Inversion*. In one scene, set in the early 1980s, the two main characters, both vacationing students, are bumping along a track in a dilapidated Morris Minor with the radio on. The track playing was 'Making Plans for Nigel' and it sounded just as fresh and vibrant then as it did when it was first released and indeed as it does now. Musically, it was just perfect for the scene, recollecting visions of endless summers and a carefree existence. But whoever had chosen this track to accompany the scene had been clever, as the lyric actually relates to the curtailing of youthful irresponsibility with staid 'plans' for a future in the real world for the unfortunate Nigel. In Rendell's book, the characters are about to find out what growing up entails. Quite recently, I was gratified to note that 'Making Plans for Nigel' was voted into a top list of punk/new wave singles in a music magazine, so you see, I can also use lists to prove anything I like as well as the next man.

I had stumbled on XTC, quite by accident, by turning the radio on in the middle of a live session by the band, promoting their debut LP 'White Music', and thought it interesting, but not compulsive. It was only later that, when returning a faulty record (again), I decided to exchange it for something else and chanced on the aforesaid XTC debut. This fortuitous purchase started me on a brief affair with the band which lasted up to about the album 'English Settlement' or thereabouts when we parted company, but during that time I enjoyed 'Drums and Wires' and 'Black Sea' enormously. It was the combination of Chamber's highly inventive drumming and the originality of the Partridge and Moulding writing partnership (Twin Towers!) that set them above the pack during that odd period when punk was trying to grow up and only succeeding in turning into new romanticism.

By now, however, the awful truth was beginning to materialise. Conversations like the one described above and others like it made me realise that this is what happens when you give up student days and enter the real world of work – and it was a bit of a shock. It was as if that record collection that had been lovingly built up ceased to exist the moment you put a suit on. All my life, some twenty years, I had been surrounded by people who had been interested in music, either by design or because, generally people under twenty were attuned to popular culture, but this was different. It dawned on me that, up to now, I had been living in a false world where I was in the majority and those that knew nothing about the recent punk explosion were the outcasts but in this environment, I was that outcast. In the real world, nobody was the slightest bit interested in the trivia of the album chart or whether Simon Le Bon had a naff haircut, except me.

There was a particularly pivotal moment that underlined the attitude of my fellow colleagues. At one point, I had cut out from the NME, an itinerary detailing dates for a UK tour by Siouxsie and the Banshees and stuck it on my in tray for reference. One senior colleague, with cold deliberation, tore the paper in half and placed it in the bin then left without a word. It was now abundantly clear that most others were obsessed with work, business and promotion, and the sort of adult conversation that bored me silly. I found that, suddenly I was looking at a lifetime in exile, cut adrift from the things I held dear. I needed a confederate, but would I find one?

Having left University, I had started a job in the property department of that bastion of institutional conservatism, the Prudential Assurance Company in Holborn, London. This entailed a rail journey from St Albans into St Pancras and then on by rattling underground to Holborn with a final walk along the bustling High Holborn to the vast red brick gothic monolith that was the Prudential's headquarters. Joining the Prudential in the late 1970s was a bit like entering a club that was a cross between a public school and the civil service. Even the inside of this Waterhouse designed building resembled a school with its endless oak panelled corridors and stone flagged staircases. Pictures of various characters from the Company's past adorned the walls and you felt if you looked closely you might find an honours board with columns of old boys listed for inspection. Rank was paramount and the entitlements included, in reverse order of seniority, a screened desk, a glass-panelled office, a wood-panelled office and tea and biscuits served from a trolley at three o'clock. Promotions were handed out on one specific day every year like a sort of school prize giving for effort, the recipient being given a discreet nod to attend the chief's office at a certain time where the award would be handed out. Given this utterly staid environment, it was, therefore, all the more astounding that, along with others, a fully war-painted and hair-spiked punkette should be taken on in our department, as temporary clerical staff for a few weeks one summer.

I can't remember her name but I do recall that with her red and green spiked hair, black make-up and nose ring, she stood out like a Belisha beacon in a sea of grey suits, without it seeming to bother her one jot. The office was agog and the poor girl was the subject of sidelong glances and whispered asides for most of her day. I began to wonder what on earth she was doing at a place like the Prudential. I always thought punks didn't work, but hung around street corners looking surly. Nothing seemed to be making sense anymore – I was stranded in a life bereft of musical conversation and now I was surrounded by working punks. It was a bit like one of those dream sequences you get in the middle of a psychological thriller where the victim is in a state of paranoia and everyday things seem sinister and forbidding. Despite her own rather surly nature (at least that seemed right), we struck up a passing acquaintance through our mutual interest in things musical. We even shouted a few words to each other at a chance meeting at an evening gig at the Lyceum featuring those purveyors of gothic gloom, the Sisters of Mercy. Whilst I felt a little awkward being seen fraternising with this rather exotic creature, it was actually rather comforting to have someone to talk to about such high brow subjects as the Ruts' and the Vibrators' latest singles. Before she left at the end of her allotted two weeks, she came over to me and asked, 'What are you *doing* here?' What indeed.

My middle class – must get a good job and stick to it – upbringing didn't really equip me to answer that one, so I stayed on for the next nine years while I tried to rationalise it, before jumping ship. During that time, I acquired a reputation for being 'that one that reads the NME and keeps going on about bands and artists we've never heard of'. Whilst it is true that my stock was not enhanced by a number of tips for success that dwindled to nothing, one of my better predictions was the rise of Martha and the Muffins, a Canadian band led by the two Marthas, Johnson and Ladly and driven by the Gane brothers. I had first encountered this band when they had played the Nashville, a well-known west London music pub in the 1980s and had enthused about their energetic powerpop to the usual disdain. However, when 'Echo Beach' suddenly assaulted the charts followed by the lesser success of the follow up single, 'Saigon', my ravings took on a slightly less manic appearance and my reputation as a man in the know rose a few points.

Another of those that I was prone to go on about was Kate Bush. Nobody who heard 'Wuthering Heights' when it was first released is unlikely to forget it. That weird lyric and complex melody, delivered in that squeaky voice was quite extraordinary and I immediately felt that this was a person who would feature strongly in a future 'Barking Mad' category and was therefore worth getting to know. I bought her first three albums, which contained some eccentric but commercially acceptable songs, but then in 1982 she released 'The Dreaming' and suddenly this strange woman was making seriously good but deeply impenetrable music. The album was not a commercial success, which is almost inevitable for work as challenging as this, but I loved it, well most of it anyway. There were sections of it that even I found difficult to fathom, but the inventiveness and creativity was manna to my jaded palette. It remains one of my favourite albums even though there are still parts of it that I find incomprehensible – perhaps that's the lure.

Following the commercial failure of 'The Dreaming', nothing more was heard for three long years. I surmised that this was the end and that the hard world of commerce had done for her but then, in 1985 a new single appeared. It was

'Running up that Hill' and it was magnificent. Over a semi-military drum beat, which for some reason always reminded me of the French Revolution and squalling synthesisers, which didn't ran a deceptively simple melody in standard verse-chorus progression. The whole thing built in intensity by the addition of more and more instruments and by the end left you feeling a bit breathless, as it seemed to close in on you in a relentless fashion. It appeared that Kate had managed to guild her singular eccentric style with a more commercial edge hence giving the listener the best of both worlds, something that all the best artists manage to do at some point in their career unless you are David Bowie, in which case you managed it for most of the time.

With all this in mind and having sought out a few of my marginally more enlightened colleagues, I dared to mention that this was a triumphant return for Ms Bush and that the forthcoming 'Hounds of Love' album could well be a classic, only to receive the reply that it was OK and what was all the fuss about. This was probably a reasonable assertion based on the fact that she had been out of the public eye for nigh on four years since the last successful single, but this attitude encapsulated my dilemma and that was nobody ever agreed with me and I was beginning to lose my sense of perspective. Was everything really rubbish? Was I acting under the delusion that my critical faculties were intact? It was becoming difficult to tell. What I really needed was an informed sounding board and eventually it came.

My job required me to manage the Company's portfolio of commercial investment properties in certain areas of the UK. Every few years, personnel were moved around and given new areas and this is what happened to me sometime in the mid 1980s. I was to be given Putney, south London as one of my new domains and I duly organised a trip there with the then incumbent, a guy named Julian, so as to spy out the land and exchange notes about ownerships and current issues. We had hardly spoken prior to this excursion, so our journey on the District underground line was largely uneventful and comprised mainly wary small talk about work. The morning was spent wandering around a sunny Putney getting a feel for the commercial and residential layout of the place and picking out those properties owned by the Prudential. By midday, hot and tired from our exertions we decided to adjourn to a pub by the river for lunch and it was in this largely unpromising venue that a chink of light entered my world. We ordered a couple of pints and a sandwich and ensconced ourselves at a table near an unseasonal fire. As usual, I couldn't help noticing that a music tape playing in the background included some quite interesting stuff, and spent rather too much time listening to it. Most of our desultory conversation passed me by as I strained to hear what was playing until my companion, who also seemed to be a little distracted said, 'What's this, then?'

'I think it's supposed to be ham.'

'No, not that! This track, who's it by?'

'Oh! I'm not sure. I think it's Lene Lovich.'

'No, must be Toyah or somebody. Another pint?

'Thanks. Are you sure it's not Lene Lovich?'

Blimey! I was so out of practice at this sort of thing that I felt a little ill at ease. Was this just small talk or were we really having a proper music conversation that may lead to all sorts of subjects including a discussion about the emergence of some unlikely lot calling themselves the Smiths? Two more pints arrived and the pub tape developed into a low-key competition to see who could identify each song first. In between, we slowly developed our new found common ground by introducing a few music-based questions into the conversation and it was then that the defining moment arose. The following question was innocently tossed my way, 'What's the significance of the Rolling Stones' single 'Brown Sugar'?'

And it was at this moment that I guessed that this was the tester. This was his way of ascertaining whether I was serious and we could pass on to that Smiths discussion or whether I was just passing the time. I felt that I had to get it right or a sane contemplation of 'This Charming Man' may never happen. I dug deep, but the trouble was, I couldn't think what the answer could be. Flaming typical! You wait years for this type of opportunity and when it arrives, it defeats you. I racked my brain trying to think of something sensible. Nothing. The exasperating thing was, I even owned the damn record! I could see it in my mind's eye with that ghastly yellow label with the red tongue logo on it... the tongue... that was it!

'It was the first Stones release on their own Rolling Stones record label'

'That's right!'

At closing time, we fell out, squinting into the bright afternoon sunlight and walked up Putney High Street to critically examine the shopping pattern. The remainder of the afternoon went:

Julian: 'We own half that Marks and Sparks on a long lease with a geared ground rent. The tenancy comes up next year, so you'll need to serve the s25 Notices soon.'

'Hmm. Fancy coming back to my place to listen to records?

'OK.'

And we did.

We have been friends ever since, though marriages and families have dented our music listening time, and still discuss the vagaries of the pop music world in our middle age like the two grumpy old men that we are. What's more, the Smiths' single 'This Charming Man' was voted a hit by our newly formed critical panel and the debut album was duly purchased.

I have always felt rather aggrieved that the Smiths were labelled with the 'miserable' tag as the majority of their work was anything but. DJs and those in the music business, like politicians, are always extremely keen to speak out about things that they don't fully understand and are quick to pigeonhole acts in a manner that does no favours to the recipient but everything to further their own publicity.

Granted, Morrissey's vocal delivery is often mournful, but intelligent examination of his lyrics often reveals a wry humour and gentle leg-pulling of the subjects rather than a more depressive stance. In the same way that cartoons like, say, Tom and Jerry, exaggerate violence in order to create comedy, so Morrissey's lyrics often exaggerate the humiliations of life in order to make a point in a light-hearted way. You would think that 'Heaven Knows I'm Miserable Now' is confirmation of the general view that the Smiths are a generally morbid lot, but actually it is the cartoon-like depiction of a grim reality that makes the song so poignantly amusing. Quite the reverse to that which some commentators would have us believe. In addition, I would defy anyone not to emerge from hearing Morrissey's achingly funny self-depreciation in 'Half a Person' without a smile on their face.

Certainly, there is no doubt in my mind that the writing partnership of Morrissey and Marr was one of this country's finest. Morrissey's pointed, conversational lyrics and down to earth imagery touched his listeners like very few others and Marr's musical acumen complemented this perfectly. Johnny Marr had a knack of making each song the equivalent of a window into a much bigger musical picture. I always had the uncomfortable feeling that when a Smiths' song started, it had actually been playing for a minute or two previously and that, as a listener, I had joined it a little late so that a phrase at the beginning of a verse was already half completed when it began. It was a strange experience to listen to these odd melodic shapes that were a little off kilter but always intriguing. More surprising is their music's proximity to the dance culture. If asked to compile a list of great dance bands, my guess would be that the Smiths would not feature highly, if at all, yet there are some in their repertoire that are real toe tappers. One in particular is 'Big Mouth Strikes Again' which barrels along in a fashion almost guaranteed to spark the weariest of bones, especially in the instrumental breaks where Marr's disco rhythm guitar and Andy Rouke's immaculate bass lines up the ante considerably – but then I can't dance so perhaps I'm misleading you here.

So for the remaining few years of my time at the Pru, I had a confederate, someone I could talk to about music without fearing universal condemnation. It was not quite like before, but it would certainly do and life could go on. Interestingly, it turned out that we have almost complementary tastes. His initial inspiration came from the likes of Bowie, Roxy and Sparks whereas I am more of a progrock devotee and this mirrors exactly the two-year age difference between us. Whereas my formative years were 1970–74 when the progressive music genre was at its height, his were slightly later during the period 1972–76 when the glam rock scene had begun to take hold. It is sobering to realise how marginal are the circumstances that shape our destiny. The differences in our respective outlooks have produced some heated debates over the years (no mention shall be made of the sampling discussion that almost came to blows in a certain Henley restaurant) but have also resulted in an exchange of references. In the light of my views about keeping music live, no one else could have persuaded me that New Order's use of tapes on stage was a legitimate art form.

With hindsight, it is easy to see that those years at the Prudential were the worst I ever endured and that what I didn't know was that, surprisingly, as I became older, I would meet more furtive pop music fans than ever. Hope I don't die before I get old, as someone didn't say.

Chapter Eighteen

SIGN OF THE TIMES

As I have already described, my love affair with the vinyl record started as a sensual attraction through touch and smell and then graduated to an appreciation of what was held between its grooves. It was therefore with some sadness that, in 1989, I finally resisted its charms and succumbed to the new disc on the block; the Compact Disc.

So having taken the plunge and bought a shiny new CD player, I then set about casting around for some shiny new discs to play on it. Usually I have a list (obviously) of 'wants & possibles' that I carry around with me. This list is augmented whenever I hear something I like or when I have read a review in a paper or magazine for something that seems promising. After a lifetime of buying music, I have developed a sixth sense that tells me what to buy and amazingly this often works well resulting in a warm glow of pleasure when a speculative purchase turns out to be a future favourite. Predictably, there is also a downside and a shelf full of played once only discs is a sad testament to the fact that no system is infallible. Unfortunately, at the point when the CD player was sitting at home waiting there was nothing on my list, probably for the first time ever, so I was forced into the unusual position of having to buy something against my better judgement. After much deliberation, I ended up buying the following three:

1. 'We Too are One' – Eurythmics

I had heard 'Sweet Dreams (are made of this)' back in 1983 and without knowing anything about Eurythmics, had invested in the album of the same name. The overriding impression I gained from this LP was of a singer of immense talent and I became a big admirer of Annie Lennox. To me, she is a rare natural performer in a profession that, surprisingly, doesn't always harbour such talent. She will sing for example, unprompted during chat shows and I have seen her do this, quite effortlessly and unaffectedly as if it were the most natural thing in the world. Yet there are those, who promote themselves as singers, that will only mime on music shows designed to showcase their talent. There is a small pool of genuine performers and I place people like Elton John and Robbie Williams in it with her. I continued to buy Eurythmics albums for a time but had lapsed by this point so this was a purchase for old times sake and accordingly it turned out to be no better than average. By this stage they were past their peak and it shows.

2.   'A Night To Remember' – Cyndi Lauper

I always felt a little sad for Cyndi Lauper for two reasons. First, she had burst onto the scene in 1984 with 'Girls Just Want to Have Fun' and had followed it up with the exquisite 'Time after Time', but was unfortunate in that, at the same time, one Madonna Ciccone was starting out and everyone else was immediately put in the shade. Second, Cyndi is a talented writer but is primarily a performer of staggering intensity. She puts her heart and soul into every performance as if her life depended on it and her stage shows can be mesmerising. As far as the great buying public is concerned, however, her exaggerated, kooky image has worked against her in the popularity polls. Why this should be, in an industry full of larger than life characters, is a little bewildering but it does seem to be the case. Again, I was a lapsed buyer of her work by this stage but felt this deserved a try. It does contain a blistering version of 'I Drove All Night', originally covered by Roy Orbison and her original version of 'Unconditional Love' which would be a minor hit for ex-Bangle Susanna Hoffs, and whilst the intensity was still there, overall it was a little disappointing.

3. 'Everything' – Bangles

The Bangles are a favourite band of mine and I have all their LPs from 'All over the Place' onwards, including this one. Their brand of updated 1960s psychedelia is a clever modernisation of an old style in a way that appeals to a new generation of listeners. But they are foremost, what I would call a 'real' band in that they are all competent instrumentalists and songwriters, great fun to see live and most of all, they all sing beautifully solo or together in harmony. Whilst Susanna Hoffs is the most recognisable vocalist and appears on most of their single releases, all four of them sing lead on album tracks and could be a lead singer in their own right. This makes their harmony singing sublime whether it's on record or live. And this is why I broke my own rule on day one. The rule was: no purchases of CD albums that I already owned on vinyl. Of course, as everybody knows, this sort of posturing never lasts and now I own nearly sixty duplications. If truth be told, the real reason why I bought this was to test the CD against the original vinyl version to see if there was any improvement in sound quality, as promised in all the advertising blurb. I hoped that this would be so in order that I could enjoy one of my favourite bands in glorious digital.

I was quite late in embracing the new digital technology as CDs and CD players had been around for several years prior to my conversion, but I had held back on the advice from some quarters that the promised improvements in sound quality had not been realised. Sadly there proved to be substance to these arguments. On playing my Bangles albums simultaneously and toggling between the LP and CD versions, there was no discernible difference in sound quality at all. What CD provided was a hiss and crackle free sound, but not a fundamentally better sound. So much for the 'perfect sound, forever' advertising slogan that Philips had peddled on the release of CD. A graphic realisation that CD was not all it was cracked up to be came years later when I was able to hear a cheap CD player up against a medium price record deck. The record sounded better in every respect. So where does this leave us?

I think we have to be careful about how these observations are interpreted. In terms of absolute sound quality, it appears that the vinyl disc is not any worse, and may be deemed better by some, than the equivalent CD, but in order to realise that sound quality, a vinyl record must be played on ruinously expensive, top of the range equipment. What CD has done is bring good quality sound to the less expensive end of the market and this process will continue as technology becomes cheaper. Inevitably, recording techniques have improved since the launch of CD so current discs are more likely to sound better than their equivalent vinyl. What CD has also done is remove the surface noise from recordings and to minimise the incidence of damage related sound degradation. But, and here is the clincher, the benefits of CD do not stop at sound quality and include convenience and compatibility. CDs can be browsed in the manner of a computer disc so that single songs may be picked at will and they can be moved between home, car and personal players with ease.

So, a resounding victory for CD? Not quite. There are other factors that have not translated quite as well as anticipated. For example, on holding a vinyl record (carefully of course) and perusing the printed-paper labels the following information can usually be found:

1. The name of the artist
2. The name of the album
3. The names of all the songs on the album
4. The name of the writer of each song
5. The name of the music publisher
6. The date the songs were published
7. The name of the record company
8. The catalogue number of the recording
9. The producer of the album

If, by some appalling misfortune, the record sleeve was lost, virtually all you need to know about the album is contained very neatly on the record label. It is the sort of information that music obsessives thrive on and it seeps into your brain every time the record is picked up. Now try finding all that information on a CD and, with the exception of some very early CDs, I will guarantee that in virtually all cases it will be either missing or incomplete. Even to find it all in the little CD booklet is a trial of Herculean stature as either it will be printed over some arty design and therefore illegible or it will be in print so small that it requires an electron microscope to view it. Most of my formative years were spent reading record labels and this has allowed me to build up a good working knowledge of popular music for what is really, very little effort. It interested me to know who wrote or produced the songs as it led to recognition of styles and idiosyncrasies. After a time, the names of performers, writers and producers would crop up time and again in different situations and a mental cross-referencing begins to take shape. This accumulation of knowledge and appreciation of effort is one of the joys of record collecting and having an interest in popular culture. I wonder whether this would have happened if I had grown up in the CD age, or, more to the point, the MP3 age?

The next issue that becomes noticeable when switching from record to CD is that the playing time of CDs is generally longer. Limited by the amount of space on an LP record and by the width of the grooves, albums tend to play for about 18–20 minutes per side. Some extend to 25 minutes, but the volume and quality of the sound deteriorates with increased length as the grooves are necessarily packed closer together. CDs have a playing time of some 77 minutes, equal to approximately 4 sides of vinyl. This has led to artists releasing longer works on CD than they would normally have done on vinyl. From my own observations, I estimate that current CD albums have an average playing time of 45–55 minutes, equivalent to about three sides of vinyl, although some are much longer – up to 60 or more minutes. One effect of this lengthening of playing time is that the listener becomes disorientated, then bored and rarely listens to the whole album in one sitting. I myself have several CDs where I have never reached the final few tracks and probably never will as a kind of apathy sets in after about half an hour.

Researchers tell us that the average attention span is about 20 minutes and tellingly, this is about the playing time of one side of a vinyl LP. When playing a vinyl record, the listener will place it on their turntable and then be aware that the stylus moves across the playing surface from outer edge towards the label. One of the advantages of listening to an LP was that the listener has a visual idea of the length of the recording. The album is divided into two sides with known playing times so that there is a discernible mid point to the proceedings (that is, when the record is turned over) and the disc itself acts as a gauge showing the listener in very visual terms exactly how far through a particular song they are and also how far through the side or half they are. This gives the listener a tangible sense of progression and a clue as to when it will end hence allowing the brain to adjust to the length of the performance.

A CD by contrast disappears into its player and gives very little clues at all. The listener is forced to set out on the journey without much indication as to where the tracks end, where the half way point is nor when it will end. This makes the experience too open ended and in frustration we switch off prematurely. For example, Moby's 'Play' is over 1 hour long and contains 18 songs. Much as I like it, I have real trouble getting to grips with this album, as I never know where I am within it and can't work out which track is which. A CD does not help the listener to break down the running order into smaller digestible chunks in the way that a vinyl record does. The read out on the CD player gives us some clues such as the track number, the total time elapsed and the track time elapsed but only one read out is possible at a time and it takes an effort to fiddle with the remote to gain all the information we need.

In the days of vinyl records, the double album was almost universally derided as an overlong indulgence and the general view was that most of them comprised a good single album padded out with filler or substandard material to fill four sides. Yet today, artists are releasing CDs that in terms of playing time are equivalent to at least an LP and a half and no one complains. However, I would contend that there is a distinct lack of quality control operating in such releases and what we are paying for is a good single album plus 10 to 15 minutes of padding. This is another reason why I find it difficult to listen to entire CDs: not only are they too long but there are too many substandard tracks. I would much rather listen to 35–40 minutes of top-notch music than I would plough through 45–55 or more minutes of variable quality product.

A vinyl album also has a structure to its running order so that the whole musical set has a shape and feeling of commencement, middle and end. The physical fact that a record has two sides allows the artist to split the set into two parts if they so desire. There are numerous combinations that have been tried such as short songs/long songs, fast songs/slow songs, songs by one writer/songs by another, vocal/instrumental and so on. The fact that Bob Marley's 'Exodus' is divided by LP side is of importance to the effect of the album. One side contains dense political protest and the other, life affirming feel-good songs. This distinction is completely lost on the purchaser of the CD version.

The running order of the songs is of vital importance. Ian McDonald, in his vastly entertaining volume 'Revolution in the Head', tells of how it took John Lennon, Paul McCartney and George Martin 24 hours of non-stop tinkering to finalise the running order of the Beatles (White) Album. When contemplating a running order, it is important to realise that the pivotal points in the set are the beginnings and ends of the record's sides. Generally, an LP will start side 1 with a perky up-tempo number to get it off to a good start and make the listener want to hear more. It is interesting to note that single releases taken from albums are often track 1 as they are the catchiest of the bunch and will attract the listener's attention. The next crunch point is the final track on side 1 which is generally the best ballad or the most unusual song. This will stay in the mind whilst the record is turned over and we are into side 2 which, again will probably start with one of the better songs in the set. The most impressive song is often saved till last, be it ballad or rocker.

But the subtleties of creating a running order must also extend to allowing each side of the record to stand by itself, hence allowing the listener to play just one side and still have a sense of beginning and closure. Clearly this could have disturbing side effects if there is no closure after one side as I experienced when occupying a bedroom next to my sister in the family home. She had borrowed my copy of Talking Heads 'More Songs about Buildings and Food' which would then be played at every opportunity. The problem was that she would only ever play side 1 and until I managed to wrest it back some time later, I hadn't a clue what was on side 2. But more alarming was the fact that by being forced to listen to one side only I experienced a sense of displacement that was increasingly unnerving. Perhaps less squeamish regimes could utilise this effect in the torture of dissidents. I'm sure repeated plays of only one side of a vinyl LP would do the trick after a few hours.

To see how this running order business works, have a look at 'Rumours' by Fleetwood Mac, one of the best selling albums of all time, as it conforms almost exactly to the plan described above. Side 1 starts with 'Second Hand News' a boisterous up-tempo romp and ends with Christine McVie's soulful ballad 'Songbird'. Side 2 opens with 'The Chain', another tour de force known to everyone who used to watch formula one motor racing on the BBC and ends with Stevie Nicks' 'Gold Dust Woman'. This last track appears at first sight to be a little underwhelming for what is supposed to be the impressive final track of the album but on closer listening reveals itself to be an understated, yet ideal closer in that it grows in intensity as the song progresses and then leaves on a climactic repeated fade. This sort of drawn-out ending is very risky as it either invokes the listener to think 'For God's sake, shut up and end' or 'Don't stop, I'm enjoying this'. In this instance, I think Fleetwood Mac got it right – several million listeners can't be wrong?

To give credit where it is due, the best ever final track on an album may well be 'A Day in the Life' from the Beatles' Sgt. Pepper. It is difficult to think of anything that is quite as life affirming.

In conclusion, the CD scores highly on cleanliness of sound, damage limitation, convenience and ability to pick single tracks at will, but it has no recognisable structure that helps the listener to remember the songs, nor does it impart any information about our musical heritage or the people that made it. There is a distinctly cultureless and materialistic flavour to the modern CD that for all its attributes is hard to ignore. Put some of these factors together, that is, the long playing time, lack of structure and ease of track picking and what listeners, including myself are turning into are musical grazers. I now find that I hardly ever listen to a complete CD because it is too long so I resort to cherry picking the best tracks and then move on to something else. It seems that time has turned back onto itself and that the music buying public is now more interested in single songs than whole albums, just as their forbears were in the 1960s when the singles chart dominated and albums were just collections of singles. With the advent of MP3, iPods and downloading from the Internet where individual songs can be purchased for less than £1, this trend is strengthening and I see no reason why it should not continue. Yet paradoxically, sales of CD singles are falling and this can only be attributed to cost. An album can be bought currently for let's say, £9–10 and this may contain 12 tracks making each song worth about 75 pence, yet singles sell for up to £3 and contain little more than one song together with several remixes or live versions of old material. It is more cost effective to buy the album and only play four tracks from it.

Like most things in life, we have accepted improvements in some areas only to lose them in others. It is for the individual to decide whether the trade off is correct and en masse to vote with our purchasing power. In this context the CD album looks safe for the moment but downloading is likely to sound the death knell for the singles market in its present form. But as we have come to recognise, technology opens new doors at an ever increasing speed so perhaps there is no reason to mourn the passing of old formats.

Chapter Nineteen

YOU'VE GOT A FRIEND

It is 6.29 am on a Wednesday morning sometime in the late 1990s and I am deep asleep. Beside me on my bedside cabinet is a clock radio pre-programmed to welcome me to the new day with the gentle strains of LBC radio at precisely 6.30 am.

Click. 'DUH DUH DA DUH DUM DUM DUM THE ACE OF SPADES THE ACE OF SPADES...'

I am now awake. My heart is pounding and a cold sweat chills my body.

'That was 'Ace of Spades' by Motorhead. Thanks to Nick of Clapham for that choice', the bright and breezy DJ informs me.

Yeah, thanks. Nick from Clapham is actually a work colleague of mine and this is clearly round two in a war of nerves involving a blitz of the media.

This all started a few years before when Nick was recruited to join our department and we found that there was a mutual interest in popular music which kept us amused from time to time. Also, we were both readers of 'Q' magazine, which, during that period ran a monthly page entitled 'Where are they now?' where readers were invited to nominate bands or artists that had slipped out of the public eye and Q would track them down and write a short piece on their life to date. I had always wondered what had become of my 'Carrier' discovery band, Fanny, and with some encouragement from Nick, wrote to Q with my suggestion. Months passed and nothing happened and so I assumed that my letter had been binned, along with many others, no doubt. Then, almost a year later, we were amazed to find in the latest issue, 'Where are they now – Fanny, as requested by Martin Warminger of Rickmansworth'. This was the first time I had ever seen my name in print and was chuffed to bits. Not only was this a bit of notoriety for me but it also provided a few minutes reading that I was genuinely interested to see. Obviously, Nick had been plotting his revenge for some time by bombarding radio stations with requests and now I had experienced the result. A truce was negotiated forthwith before anybody suffered a minor heart attack from being woken up by anything worse than Motorhead (although this would be difficult to imagine, Budgie notwithstanding).

By the mid 1980s, I had had enough of the Prudential's institutional atmosphere and had joined Debenham Tewson and Chinnocks (now DTZ Debenham Tie Leung), a private firm of commercial estate agents with rabbit warren offices in the West End of London. This was a good move for me as it meant I could spend the lunch hour browsing in the HMV store in Oxford Street or any of the numerous smaller music shops in Berwick Street. The office atmosphere was paradoxically both more relaxed in that the people were less staid in outlook, yet more urgent in that providing a service was paramount to the success of the firm. It was here that, as the years rolled by, I started to find a few kindred souls who were not averse to the odd musical discussion.

It is a touch ironic that when I was young and starting my first job at the Prudential, I could never find anyone amongst my work colleagues who would even admit to having an interest in pop music, yet here I am on the brink of middle age and everyone I meet of around my generation is a closet musician, concert frequenter or fan generally. It is quite extraordinary. Could it be that people of my generation have finally grown up and realised that rock music has played an important part in their lives and are now not ashamed to admit it? The fact that popular music is now part of the establishment is a contributing factor, but I can't help feeling that there are a number of band wagon jumpers who have decided it is now socially crucial to be a music fan, but where were they twenty-five years ago when the social environment was much more hostile? Certainly, from music store sales figures it appears that it is the older sections of the national demographic that are the ones buying more CD albums than any other section even if it does mean more 70s and 80s albums filling the racks at the expense of new music. Oh well, I suppose I should be grateful that at least my generation have come out of the closet but the stigma of being a music fan in later life still hangs in the air like a vengeful ghost.

As an example of a genuine case, a few years back, an IT consultant named Pete joined the Company and it was not long before we discovered our mutual interest. Not only is Pete a fellow obsessive, he plays real guitar in a real band of 'definitely on the wrong side of forty' musicians and has a teenaged daughter who is striving to make a name for herself as 'Toy', the bass player in a female trio; The Faders. In true modern style, The Faders have their own flashy website with audio and video samples, biographies and the like and have already hyped their way onto various television music shows. I wish her luck in this new image is everything media-driven world.

Away from the office, this was the time of the Great Pub Idea. Julian and I with his friend Frog (don't ask) would often meet for a drink and the three of us would muse about topics of the day. One idea from these alcohol fuelled brainstorming sessions was the Great Headline Competition. This involved us attending a concert and then attempting to guess a suitable NME type headline for a fictitious review of the band's performance. This was meant as a bit of fun for us, but there was one occasion where it had unfortunate consequences. We had just been to see The Cure in concert at Wembley Arena and after the event, were indulging in the usual ritual of composing our headlines when it fell to me to invent something pithy. At the time, one of the highlights of the Cure's set was the song 'A Forest' from their album

'Seventeen Seconds'. I have played this recently, for the first time for some years, and was struck with how atmospheric it sounds. The gated drum sound, phased cymbals, ghostly synthesisers and steely, heavily chorused guitar together with Robert Smith's plaintive voice reminded me how inventive and different they once sounded. Taking my cue from this song and remembering that Goodies episode, I submitted 'A Walk in the Black Forest' as my review headline thinking that this nicely summed up their slightly depressive tone and stately pace. We all smiled at our respective entries, patted ourselves on the back for our unparalleled wit and promptly forgot all about it, as usual.

The following Wednesday lunchtime, I collected my copy of the NME from the newsvendor on Great Marlborough Street and was ambling back to the office when I happened to turn to the Live Reviews page. There, staring out from the page was a review of the Cure at Wembley under the headline, yes, I'm afraid so; 'A Walk in the Black Forest'. I think about three people walked into me before I became aware of my surroundings again and hurried back to my desk. Later, I spoke to Julian about my new career in journalism and was then informed that Frog had been reading the NME whilst waiting on the station platform for his train. It was at the very moment when the train arrived that he had spotted the headline and, in a daze of amazement, let the doors shut and the train leave the station before realising that he had missed it and would be late for his work appointment. The competition was quietly dropped thereafter.

The 1980s was the Thatcher decade of prosperity (for some) and wealth creation and so not to be left out, I took advantage of the events that unfolded when, as luck would have it, the firm I had just joined changed its status from private to public and applied for a listing on the London stock exchange. As an employee, I was entitled to apply for preferential shares on the day of listing, so, alerted to the fact that there may be money to be made, took out a bank loan and sent in my application. The shares were offered at £1.70

each and on the day of floatation, the stock market price rose to £2.10 at which point I sold my entire allocation, thus securing a 23% profit on my outlay. This exercise provided the means to embark on a plan that I had harboured ever since that day with Steven Rodford – to write and record my own songs.

My capitalist windfall allowed the purchase of an electric guitar, a digital drum machine and the best prize of all, a four-track portastudio. A portastudio was the toy all musicians coveted and was once so futuristic that it had even been featured on 'Tomorrow's World' where a game Michael Rod had demonstrated its capabilities with a selection of guitars, live in the studio. In essence, it comprised a machine that used standard audio cassettes but had a much more sophisticated control of the recording and playback process. By way of explanation, a cassette tape allows four music tracks to be recorded onto it – two tracks in one direction (for left and right stereo channels for side 1) and two tracks in the other direction when the tape is turned over to play side 2. A portastudio operates by recording on all four tracks in the same direction so that the tape has only a single side, but more importantly it allows each track to be recorded separately without erasing the others. Then, when all four tracks have been recorded, they can be played together using a rudimentary mixer, revealing the finished product. This is ideal for songwriters as it means that a vocals, drums, guitar and bass can be recorded one at a time and played back together forming the completed song. In fact, more parts can be added with a bit of technical wizardry, but we need not go into that here. Once I had obtained a microphone and borrowed a bass guitar from my brother, I was in business.

At first, I looked through my old songs from my university days to see if there was anything worth recording and picked out one or two of the more promising candidates. First, I gave them a much-needed makeover and in some instances, rewrote either melody or lyrics. Then began the long process of programming the drum machine, working out the bass and guitar parts and rehearsing them and then recording. The first thing I discovered about recording, even in the privacy of your own home with no one there to see you, is that no matter how well you rehearse something, as soon as the tape is running, you tense up like a taut rope in the face of a machine that knows nothing except how to keep a metronomic beat and you make loads of mistakes. After a short learning curve, I gave up rehearsing in earnest as being too time consuming and just set about doing as many takes as it took before one worked without a major blunder. This is what happens when the creative urge strikes – you need to do things quickly before it disappears even if this means coming to terms with slightly substandard results. On the positive side, less rehearsal usually meant coming up with something new without thinking about it, which was great as long as it all worked, musically.

The second aspect of recording alone is the sheer time involved in bringing a three-minute song to fruition. The hours it takes to write a song, arrange it, create all the instrumental parts and rehearse them all, record all the parts and finally mix the results into the finished product, is mind boggling. I began to understand how Mike Oldfield must have felt about half way through side one of recording 'Tubular Bells' on his own. A form of recklessness creeps up on you and you yearn to get the thing finished by any means and rush through the remaining processes, letting standards slip and cutting corners indiscriminately. Unfortunately, this desperation then proceeds to stare back at you from the tape forever more. Thus after a period of concentrated and increasingly frenzied effort, the songs would magically come to life as layer upon layer of sound was added. But the one aspect that never failed to be uplifting was to finally hear the completed work, irrespective of standard. There is nothing quite like it.

It was then that I saw an advert in a recording magazine for a Roland Juno 6 synthesiser going cheap. Analogue keyboards such as this were now old technology and this was a good opportunity to add some new sounds to my recordings at a bargain price. Those who know about early synthesisers will recognise the Juno 6 as the classic pre-digital keyboard – the one without any preset sounds but loads of sliders, knobs and buttons with which to create your own sounds, even if they did all sound strangely similar. Accordingly, I spent a day driving down to Ashford in Kent to meet the owner, do a bit of bargaining over price and then return with the instrument. All I had to do now was learn to play it.

In fact, in my usual impetuous way, I only ever got as far as learning how to play three finger chords and the odd one-handed melody or bass line, but it was sufficient just to add some colour to the basic guitar bass and drum set-up. From then on all my recordings had lush keyboard chords in the bits that needed a bit more drama.

Eventually, having run out of the sort of material I considered good enough and needing some more songs to record, I started to look to other artists as inspiration and try and write in the style of say, Madonna or Phil Collins. Funnily enough, whatever I came up with never sounded anything like the original template, which was probably just as well but it did indicate how difficult it is to copy someone else's style exactly without sounding like a particularly bad pastiche. One idea I was really interested to try was to write something based around Tina Weymouth's bass style for Talking Heads.

Ever since I had bought Talking Heads' debut album, '77' on the basis of its attractive red sleeve, I had admired their style and by the time that 'More Songs about Buildings and Food' was released, I was a firm fan of Tina's bass playing. There was something about the way she put together these little staccato runs of very few, but harmonically telling, notes that fascinated me. Together with husband, drummer Chris Frantz, they formed as tight a rhythm section as you would care to hear, which was all to the good when David Byrne's vocal and guitar style were much more rhythmically fluid. I saw them play live on two occasions and was spellbound by the vice-like rhythms they could produce in a live environment. Anyway, I had a go at trying to base a song around a Tina Weymouth type bass riff and spent days trying to get it right. In the end a song was written but somehow it didn't quite have the punchiness I was looking for and the reality is; it probably never would have no matter how long I toiled to achieve it. The realisation dawned that whilst it is acceptable to copy styles, you really don't want to end up sounding like the template, so a bit of variety is not a bad thing. In fact, all sorts of other possibilities open up from the basic premise, which puts your own individual stamp on it. All the best people do it but the trick is to hide your influences. It is yet another part of the 'mixing of styles to create something new' idea that pushes art forward and to copy directly is an artistically pointless exercise.

After a few years of spending much of my time writing and recording, I had amassed several tapes worth of songs of varying quality. When I listen to them now from a safe critical distance I can see that some are reasonable, some are terrible, some have good melodic ideas and most have dreadful lyrics, but they are all mine and there is a certain pride in achievement. Interestingly, although the later ones are technically more proficient and therefore sound better sonically, it is the early attempts where I didn't quite know what I was doing that often sound the best. They have a freshness and invention about them from breaking rules before I knew that rules existed and although let down by the performance or recording technique or the fact that they are musically underdeveloped, they show an originality that is not always present in later recordings. There must be a universal truth that we do our best work when we are young and unfettered by the unconscious limits that experience brings. Remember, Einstein was but 21 years old when he formulated his Theory of Relativity, but I don't remember him writing any catchy songs.

In the early days of my recording experiments, I would get together with Jerry and Ashley in their place in Redhill and we would form a makeshift band to record material that one of us had written, so it is a double disappointment that Ashley never became a rock megastar with Christer as I would now have in my possession several extremely valuable tapes of him playing bass or singing on songs we recorded before he was famous. As it is, eBay, Christie's or Sotheby's will not be troubled by me, just yet.

Picking out future stars is a perilous occupation as my Teach In debacle proves, but picking out worthwhile listening is difficult enough even from artists that have been around for some time. Like parachute jumping, it often takes an unforeseen push to enter the world of the new and unknown. When Altered Images came along with 'Happy Birthday' in the early 1980s, I really hated it for its triteness and for Clare Grogan's ludicrous persona, but then came the push. I had been offered a lift into town by a friend one evening when he decided to play Altered Images', 'Happy Birthday' on the car stereo. When I say car stereo what I really mean is the sort of equipment designed to fill a small hall with sound, but crammed into a car. At ear splitting volume 'Happy Birthday' took on a new surreal quality and it wasn't all bad. When my ears stopped ringing, the experience prompted me to explore Altered Images' other output and I found things like the sinister 'Dead Pop Stars' and the anxious 'A Days Wait' and I was hooked. Suddenly, Clare Grogan didn't seem quite so silly and the quality of the songs, particularly on their debut album was much better than could be expected from hearing 'Happy Birthday' alone. You do get the feeling that this single did them no favours despite its popularity with restaurateurs for birthday parties.

It often takes an amount of bravery to look beyond image and hype, especially in the areas of teenage cult bands, but sometimes it is worth it. The Monkees, being the original manufactured band, were cynically marketed to appeal to the young but something went wrong and despite my first single ever episode, some of the product turned out to be very good indeed. Mind you, with writers such as Neil Diamond, Carole

King and John Stewart contributing songs this was always a danger. But I would cite not just the Monkees and A-ha's 'Scoundrel Days' but also Duran Duran's 'Rio' and with certain reservations, Bananarama's eponymous 1984 offering, as above average albums by bands, who at the time were considered no more than teenage fads. In the case of the latter, this is undoubtedly due to a string of top quality songs from the pens of ace songwriters, Tony Swain and Steve Jolley ('Cruel Summer', 'Rough Justice' and 'Robert de Niro's Waiting') but then good songs are always the backbone of well received acts, almost irrespective of the performer's talent.

It always comes down to the songs. It is the reason that I liked Cliff Richard as a small child and it is the reason why I like Britney Spears today. Give me a good song and I can look past the fact that the video comprises a standard fantasy wrapped up in a marketing firm's perfect packaging for sale to consumers the world over – and I don't just mean Cliff.

Chapter Twenty

CEREMONY

It is one of those inexplicable quirks of life that the simplest ideas are often the most influential and that those produced after long periods of toil founder in a morass of complexity. So it was with the simplicity of the Top Five.

I have already alluded to the 1980s being the time of the Great Pub Idea. The second such idea to emerge from the pub conversations I had with Julian and Frog in the mid 1980s was not earth shatteringly novel, but its implementation was different and its far-reaching implications over the next fifteen years were certainly not envisaged. One night, our conversation had turned, as it often did, to that old chestnut; our favourite albums of all time and the statutory arguments about definition and content were raging. The problem with this type of argument is generally to do with knowledge, or the lack of it. It is all very well to contend that, say, Depeche Mode's 'Black Celebration' is the best album in the known universe (it isn't) but if the other panellists in the discussion have never heard it, how can there be an informed debate? What eventually happens is that the whole discussion degenerates into a slanging match of the 'my band's better than your band' variety. It was at this moment of realisation that the concept of a 'hearing' was conceived. The solution, we agreed was as follows:

Each of us would produce a Top Ten Albums of all time list, carefully defined as those albums that we owned and felt had artistic merit but perhaps not those we played the most.

We would each choose a representative track from each album in our respective lists that best displayed its worth.

We would arrange to meet at a mutually convenient location and *play* all thirty tracks (that is, ten tracks each). One track each by turns.

Some conclusion would be drawn. But even if it weren't, it would be an interesting experiment.

At the time, I was living in a grim first-floor flat conversion in a Victorian terrace in Harlesden, a particularly rundown part of northwest London, with views over the marshalling yards of Willesden Junction and the power station beyond. So it was with some surprise that it was agreed that my flat would serve as the location and a date was duly agreed. As with most pub ideas, it seemed a good one at the time and it was only after the cobbled together bones of the idea sank in some days later that the cold dawn descended and the enormity of the task revealed itself. This was a 'put your LPs where your mouth is' moment and the pressure to produce a seriously good Top Ten that would be judged by your peers was simultaneously exciting and daunting, but mainly daunting. There suddenly grew a nagging temptation to rush out and buy all the known classic albums and then present them as if you had owned them for years, but this was eventually defeated. Nevertheless, it took me weeks to complete my list of ten albums whilst I consumed a forest of softwood's worth of paper but eventually I had my definitive, take on all comers list of great albums. Exasperatingly, despite the moment of the occasion and from a distance of twenty years, I can no longer remember who was in it and no written records were kept of the undertaking, but I'm sure it must have included something by The Smiths, Siouxsie, Fanny, Kate Bush, Curved Air and the other usual suspects that I have spoken of previously.

The appointed day dawned bright and sunny with clear blue skies and a gentle breeze. Exactly the sort of day not to be spent inside. Nevertheless, by ten o'clock in the morning the three of us were settled down with our thirty albums, carefully hidden so as not to give the game away too soon.

By turns each track was introduced by its sponsor, a little nervously at first but with gaining confidence as the morning progressed and was then played in an atmosphere of reverent silence. The first realisation was that thirty tracks were far too many and by lunch we had barely covered the first twelve. We repaired to the pub and reviewed progress. The unanimous view was that the undertaking was actually very good fun and lent a new slant to those albums we already knew and an introduction to those we didn't. Fuelled by alcohol, the afternoon session was, if anything, slower than the morning session as the introductions became more verbose and the mechanics of playing each track, more leisurely. By early evening, we were in serious time trouble but nevertheless decided to break in order to drop in on a party given by some ex-flatmates of mine in West Hampstead. In retrospect, this was a huge mistake. Not only did it waste valuable time but it also resulted in one of those moments that all music obsessives dread.

I had found myself talking to a girl I had known some years before and in a state of evangelistic fervour, had given her an overlong and enthusiastic description of our Top Ten day from its conception to execution only to be met on completion by utter silence and one of those glassy eyed vacant stares that said, 'What on earth are you talking about?'

Just for an instant, the world appeared to stand still. It was one of those moments of extreme clarity where your whole lifestyle is brought under a highly forensic microscope and found to be wanting in every possible way. No one but a music fanatic would even begin to consider that a whole day spent inside playing artistically credible, but occasionally unlistenable records could be described as fun, yet there I was proposing just that. We left soon afterwards.

Back in my flat, we waded through the remaining tracks and eventually called it a day late into the evening. Despite our best endeavours, no conclusions were ever drawn but there was a consensus of agreement that it was a worthwhile and enjoyable exercise that with certain modifications should be attempted again in the future. It wasn't.

Until one day several years later, when the idea surfaced in slightly different circumstances. By the end of the 1980s both Julian and I had met our future wives, Ann and Lib respectively and we would often socialise as a foursome.

I had met Lib through a fellow resident of the block of flats I inhabited in Ealing. She seemed like the sort of person who would put up with my music obsessions and just to prove the point, dashed off to see Bruce Springsteen at Wembley Stadium a few days after our first meeting in 1988 – there are some people with whom you just can't compete and the Boss is one of them. After a year or so of manoeuvring, we decided to make the ultimate commitment; to amalgamate our CD collections – even though this would put my stack of Curved Air albums dangerously close to her complete set of Phil Collins.

Following this action of intent, we married in a morning ceremony on a sunny July day in 1990 and spent a warm languid evening together at The Complete Angler, a hotel on the banks of the Thames at Marlow. Even then, the music world wouldn't leave us alone. Sipping our cocktails on the riverside patio, I became peripherally aware of a pair of legs striding past, followed by a mop of spiky hair. On a more circumspect examination it turned out that the legs belonged to Rachel Hunter and the hair to Rod Stewart, or was it the other way around? Clearly they had heard of our wedding and had turned up to keep us company, which they did through cocktails and dinner, although at a discreet distance. The atmosphere in the hotel dining room was relaxed in the way that only a sultry summer evening can be and was augmented by a pianist who tinkled away in the corner whilst everyone ignored him. But was it my imagination that he slipped in a couple of bars of 'Sailing' before quickly reverting to his originally chosen melody before you-know-who noticed? Probably not, but it would have been fun. We thought about inviting Rod back to our tenth wedding anniversary but it didn't seem quite the same when we noted that Rachel wouldn't be able to attend.

It was during one of our foursome meetings with Julian and Ann, which probably involved cocktails, that the idea arose, phoenix like, from the ashes of the original concept, but this time it would take the form of an annual awards ceremony in the manner of industry awards, but nominated by us. This was madness, but we couldn't help ourselves. It was proposed that the new concept would cover four categories:

1. Best Artist – this would be a person whom we thought had made a significant contribution to music in the previous twelve months. It need not be a single artist and could be a member of a band.
2. Best Band – this would be similar to the artist category, but for bands as a whole.
3. Best Single – This would be a genuine single, or if not, a single track from an album that was adjudged to be outstanding.
4. Best Album – this would be the best album released that year.

The four of us would nominate a winner in each category taken from the output released in the previous twelve months. Initially, it was envisaged that the nominees would merely be revealed to the others in the form of a list over dinner at a venue of our choice. Thus was born what would come to be called the 'Top Five' (although at this early stage there were only four categories) and it ran for eleven years until 2000 when it was sadly put out to grass through old age.

The first ceremony took place at Muswells restaurant, Ealing in 1989 when our category winners were revealed between courses. In practice, once the winners had been announced, the evening felt a bit flat and so, inevitably, having resurrected the idea, we couldn't resist moving future ceremonies to a venue where the winners' tracks could be played to the others. From 1990 onwards we would gather at one or other of our homes once a year to play our selections. On each occasion, in order to allow time for the participants to relax and for the mood to settle the format was amended to include a fifth category which was placed at the beginning of the proceedings. This was the 'Revisited' or 'Lest we forget' round where anything that had been released prior to the year in question could be played assuming the tenuous link that it had been rediscovered by the proposer during the previous twelve months. This round would allow us to get into the mood of the event before the serious stuff was introduced. Thus was born the Top Five, which over the proceeding eleven years would take all of us on a journey, both musically and geographically and for which we all hold a modicum of affection.

After a run of several years, the order of service and its traditions began to evolve. The importance of these traditions cannot be stressed enough and as they became set in stone, woe betide anyone who deviated from them. The following gives a fairly accurate picture of what would occur in the later years:

1. Initially, there would be a good-natured yet heated argument over the running order of the categories. This would happen, almost without fail, even after many years of doing the same event, year after year. The running order would then be agreed (again) as; revisited, artist, band, single, album. It was always important to have the album category last as this was deemed to be the most important.

2. Having agreed the running order, a cheap champagne would be served and lots drawn for the order in which the participants would reveal their choice. This was always closely monitored for cheating as no one ever wanted to go first and the favoured position of being last meant that your final choice would be the last of the evening.

3. Each person would introduce and then play their choice for the first category in the order decided by the lots. The subsequent categories would follow with an alcohol break between categories. In later years, this was augmented to the serving of chilli, although how this got started, I'll never know.

4. By the final two categories, the effects of alcohol and the occasional chilli put everyone in a mellow frame of mind and the music began to take on a surreal quality.

5. In the fourth year and thereafter, a new feature was introduced whereby each participant was allowed to play a Joker in any category. This allowed that person to play two tracks in the round, either from the same album or different albums (thereby allowing a sixth nominee in by the back door). Mostly, the Joker was reserved for the final Best Album category. Interestingly, no one ever played his or her Joker in the initial Rediscovery category.

6. After the final choice in category five, there were times when, in a state of alcohol fuelled exuberance, no one would want to stop and unless someone called a halt, more categories would mysteriously appear until we were in danger of ruining the whole evening with spurious submissions.

The entire premise for these awards rested on the fact that each participant bought at least four albums of newly released material each year and as time passed and family responsibilities increased, this became harder to guarantee. There was always the unspoken joke that eventually, we would all end up playing four tracks from the same album, one in each category. Certainly, it was known for two tracks from the same album to find their way into two different categories in times of desperation, and although this was generally frowned upon, everyone turned a blind eye in a 'there for the grace of God' sort of way.

In the way of all annual awards, be they global, national or personal, there exist the anomalies caused by the strict timescale. In some twelve-month periods, I had a wealth of fantastic material to choose from and in others next to nothing. This would result in the rejects from the good year being of better quality than the winners in the lean year and who is to say that a little massaging of the twelve-month period went on in order to move some releases into a subsequent or previous year? In fact, this very problem spawned its own awards when, for want of something better to do during the lull between year end awards, we staged a Top Five for those acts that had failed to be nominated for one reason or another.

The other, rather tragic side effect of the Top Five was that during the year between ceremonies nobody ever discussed new purchases with any of the group for fear of giving away their potential future nominations. After years of doing just that, this was hard to come to terms with and it is sad to say that for 10 years or so, Julian and I never discussed new music until the year following its release. Now that it is all over, we are back to normal – that is to say, we rubbish virtually everything without restraint.

The ceremony itself would take place in the year following the twelve-month period under review. Usually, this meant sometime after March in order to gain a degree of judgemental perspective from the year in question, especially if a flurry of purchases had been made around Christmas at the very end of the review year. In the early years there was a fair amount of moving home and the venue for this event changed annually. The inaugural event took place at Julian and Ann's flat in Henley and the following year at our new house in Ealing. In both these venues, however, we were painfully aware of the noise we were making and the proximity of neighbours.

For the third year, therefore, we took the bizarre decision to rent a detached holiday cottage in the middle of some bleak fields just outside Marlborough. I boxed up and transported all our stereo equipment with us with the intention of setting it up in the cottage thus allowing us the benefit of taking our time playing our choices in the knowledge that we could be as loud as we liked without disturbing anyone. Lib and I arrived late in the evening on a freezing February Friday after a gridlocked drive along the M4 to be met at the cottage by the owners. It was pitch dark in the field, but they had lit the log burners and the place looked inviting. As soon as I was sure they had gone, I started to unpack all the boxes of stereo equipment but having got half of them stacked up by the car, they returned unexpectedly to give us some vital information about the electricity meter. I could see their look of horror as their eyes rested on the boxes I was unloading and promptly shut the car boot and directed their attention elsewhere. They obviously thought we were involved in some dodgy deal or other involving drugs or contraband, and we half expected to be knocked up by the police at two o'clock in the morning, but to our relief, they never returned.

On inspection we found that the cottage was full of personal items, as if someone had left suddenly, like the Marie Celeste, or had just died, which was more likely. The kitchen was filthy and the beds damp, but the log fires were welcoming and by the time Julian and Ann had arrived we had cleaned enough of the kitchen to heat a pizza and open a bottle of wine. With the stereo set up in the living room and the log burners emitting that sweet smelling wood smoke we had a relaxed weekend indulging our Top Five with a few bottles of wine in the evening and during the daytime, touring the surrounding countryside.

We decided against repeating this exercise the following year in case the drugs squad turned up and so the fourth year took us back to the Henley flat and the fifth year saw us ensconced at Julian and Ann's new detached house in Long Crendon, a far more suitable venue.

In the sixth year, work had relocated Julian and Ann to a flat in Amsterdam but even this didn't deter us and Lib and I arrived on a flight from Heathrow complete with CDs ready for a European version of our tried and tested traditions. I love Amsterdam with its canals, vertical architecture and lack of cars, but in winter the temperature is generally below freezing making sightseeing a character building occupation. Nevertheless, we took in the Van Gogh museum and the parks and during one evening, treated the other tenants in the canalside residential block to our choices for that year. It was a wonderful weekend for which we owe the Top Five, at least partially, a debt of gratitude.

Thereafter, our meetings tended to gravitate towards our house in Rickmansworth until in 2000, the last rites were performed. It seemed a good time to end at the close of the millennium and anyway, by this time we were all struggling to find new things to showcase and we were all in danger of playing our Joker in the Rediscovery round, something that our dignity could not allow.

Now that five years have passed since its demise, it is time to look back on the Top Five with a cool head. Happily, the results were all recorded and reflecting on them now, I am impressed by the diversity of music that was proposed. Whilst it is true that, in general the nominees occupied the pop, rock, indie and folk genres and it is obvious that everyone had his or her favourites who tended to feature strongly, the overall spread within those limits was moderately wide. I am amused to note that the likes of Frank Sinatra and Pavarotti rub shoulders with Temple of the Dog and Marilyn Manson. There is also an enduring mix between major artists and obscure here today and gone tomorrow acts. A brief statistical analysis bears presenting here. In the eleven years that the Top Five ran, no less than 145 different bands and artists were nominated in one or other of the categories and only 48 of them were nominated more than once. The most frequently nominated were:

1. Radiohead (8 times)
2. Pearl Jam (7 times)

3. Lush, Aimee Mann, Madonna and Foo Fighters (4 times)
4. REM, Neil Young, Sinead O'Connor, The Manic Street Preachers, The Cardigans, Björk, Oasis, Dubstar, Deacon Blue, Suede, Tori Amos, Elvis Costello and Prince (3 times)
5. 29 others (twice)
6. The remaining 97 (once)

In retrospect, the Top Five acted as a fascinating forum for new ideas and sounds as well as an enjoyable social occasion. All four of us learnt something from these sessions and indeed, subsequent purchases were made of albums showcased by others. Perhaps it will be resurrected one day, but for the moment it remains a fond memory.

Chapter Twenty-One

IN THE YEAR 2525

My daughter is five years old. She owns her own portable CD player and various CDs. She knows how to load and play them, how to skip tracks and to generally find her way around the disc. She also knows how to operate our television and the video recorder and how to navigate around a DVD using various remote controls. Technology holds no fear for her. Her younger brother will grow up in the same way, taking it all in his stride. How different it all is from my own upbringing.

In the intervening years between my childhood and those of my children, popular music has become part of everyday life; so much so that we hardly notice it is there. It adds the soundtrack to every film we see at the cinema and every programme we watch on television and even the adverts and continuity between programmes. It plays in shops and restaurants, airports and football stadiums. It seems that there is no business or public place that does not use popular music as a background to its own endeavours. Many years ago, I was watching television coverage of the Winter Olympic Games when the women's individual ice dance competition started. One by one the skaters took to the ice to the accompaniment of a suitably grand piece of classical music until the Russian contestant started her routine. Expecting the usual piece of mournful Russian music, the spectators were shocked to hear The Police's 'Synchronicity II' blast out from the dreadfully inappropriate speaker system. The dance routine that complemented this song was fast and furious and soon the audience were clapping along to Stewart Copeland's storming beat and Andy Summers' complex guitar picking.

Today, I doubt that that same audience would turn a hair, so common has pop music become.

Accordingly, today's generations are partially anaesthetised to its effect and filter it out in the way that advertising is tuned out. It is hardly surprising then that music to them no longer has the excitement of something new and different. It does not appear to them that there is anything secretive or rebellious about it as adults listen to it constantly. Technological advances, too, in audio and visual media have been so great that the world I grew up in has become as far away as the Middle Ages in the perception of most of today's children.

When I was a similar age of five, our family home contained a black and white television set and a valve radio. Plugged into the back of the radio was an ancient auto-change record player cunningly built into the bottom drawer of a large chest of drawers so as to keep it out of sight. I was not allowed to touch any of this equipment until I was about eight years old when I was given permission to play records. In reality, this translated as the few singles that I owned and the family selection that I didn't. I had no LPs that I could call mine and had no urge to play the few my parents owned. Nevertheless, despite the paucity of technology I developed a skill that no child of any generation after about 1985 will ever have and that is knowledge of how to stack seven-inch vinyl singles into an auto-change record player. Believe me, it's not as easy as it sounds as I quickly discovered. Most people would assume that you just arrange half a dozen disks in a pile, one disk on top of another, locate the whole pile on the spindle, brace it with the retaining arm and switch on. Not so. Some records are warped and will only play on the top or the bottom of the pile, some are too thin and make two disks drop at once and so have to be placed in a particular position in the pile and still others will slide over the one below on the turntable making it unplayable. All these problems need to be solved when constructing a singles stack that will play in order and without slippage or speed variation. It was an all-consuming problem that required the experimental skills of a nuclear scientist and an iron will. Try telling that to youngsters today and see where you get.

The first piece of real hardware that I had to myself was built from a children's electronics set. For my eleventh birthday I was given a Philips Electronics Kit, which comprised a hardboard base with holes punched in it, a set of springs, circuit diagrams and various electronic components like transistors, capacitors and resistors (no microchips!). By laying a particular circuit diagram over the baseboard and placing springs into the holes as shown, circuits could be built up by locating the various components between the springs. In this way and with the aid of a battery, the budding electronics engineer could make burglar alarms, automatic night-lights and all manner of other fascinating projects. One of the circuit diagrams allowed the construction of a basic medium wave radio receiver and this is the configuration in which my educational toy spent most of its life, as the prospect of having Radio 1 on tap in my bedroom rather than stealing the family radio was too good to miss. Also, despite being only a makeshift job, it proved to be extremely reliable and allowed Johnny Walker's Radio 1 evening show to see me through years of homework. It also allowed illicit night-time listening without a hitch.

My patched together kit radio was finally put into retirement when, at the age of fifteen, I was able to treat myself to a trendy new transistor radio. It was a handsome beast in black plastic with a silver front grill and black leather carrying case. It was with this tiny machine that I was able to tune into Radio Luxembourg at night and listen through the earpiece as the static raged. It was also small enough to attach to my bike's handlebars for my morning paper round and other journeys to friends and the like. At that time the ownership of a radio was something to aspire to. Today, radios are the size of a credit card and come as an extra in virtually everything else you buy, so there is no real desire to own one.

After that came my own record player and eventually, at the age of eighteen, my own stereo system. My first record player was an odd affair, purchased from a catalogue run by my mother and for which I paid her something like 5 shillings (25 pence) a week for a year. Constructed almost entirely of black and grey plastic, it took the form of a briefcase which, when opened, contained a small turntable and tone arm and two removable stereo speaker boxes which could be placed either side of the case to provide stereo width. The controls comprised basic volume and tone knobs and a selector for toggling between the record player and an inbuilt radio (naturally). It sounded excruciatingly tinny, but was all mine and meant that I could listen to my own records in my own bedroom.

My daughter already has access to all these things and technology and music are part of her young life. When she was a baby, we would use music to lull her to sleep in her cot. Amazingly, and conveniently for us, there were certain songs that would soothe her instantly to silence even during the worst crying fits. The songs that revealed themselves to have this mystical power were 'Losing My Religion' by REM and anything from Madonna's 'Music' CD, although I fail to recall any such claims in the respective artists' advertising campaign. Later on, 'Baby, One More Time' by Britney Spears was also found to have this effect and was added to the emergency list for a bit of variety. If only these artists knew it, they could sell shed loads of CDs to sleepless parents the world over. It is curious how music exerts such power over us in times of emotional stress and that babies, in particular, respond to the primal messages of music. For many months, she would drift off to sleep to the sound of REM's 'Reveal' CD and we were shocked, but in retrospect not surprised, when her first uttered sentence was 'She just wants to be' – a line from track three of that album. Nor, when watching the TV comedy, The Royle Family, did it surprise us when 'Baby David' was soothed to sleep by

Radiohead's 'No Surprises' from their 'OK Computer' album. Pop music is the new Lullaby.

One other factor that became clear was that she could sense the emotional content of music from a very early age despite not understanding the majority of the lyrics. Not long after she began to speak, I was playing a Zombies CD, when amongst the generally minor key original songs came a genuine blues number, full of pain and suffering. At this point, she wanted to turn the CD player off and when questioned replied that the song was 'too scary'.

Our household has recently gained access to various music television channels and although you can only watch so many music videos before becoming glassy eyed, there is no doubt that they have reawakened my interest in singles and new artists. Clearly this is what they are designed to do and I have to admit that it has worked in one or two cases. Anastacia is one of them. I have come to like Anastacia a lot. She has a big, big voice strangely reminiscent of Tina Turner, but manages to keep it under control so as to impart the maximum of emotional effect. Her style has now stabilised into the big rock number that suits her voice so well and 'Left Outside Alone' is one of the most powerful examples to date. The accompanying album is full of big ballads and rock meets urban and sounds uncannily like the sort of album Melanie C ought to be producing but doesn't quite manage it.

And whilst on the subject of the girl powered ones, I didn't think that the Spice Girls were that bad, in spite of the vast marketing machine behind them, but the individual careers we have seen since their split have been of varying quality. Stripped of the protective shell of their collective image, each member has had to create an individual personality that will appeal to a slightly less adoring audience. Melanie C is clearly the female Bryan Adams and her undoubted talent as a singer and her brand of pop rock suits her well despite the slightly below par albums. Melanie B (or G) has developed a tough urban soul sound and Emma Bunton could be a contemporary Sandie Shaw as her girl next door image and talent for picking retro 1960s sounding songs are perfect for the part. Geri Halliwell is more than at home in the world of over the top kitsch pop and has excelled in this genre, which leaves Victoria Beckham whose obvious musical style is – don't tell me – hmm.

And there, I think, lies the problem for the former posh spice – she really doesn't have an obvious affinity for any musical style and it's far too late to start looking for one now. It almost begs the question; what type of music does she, herself like?

Another band that the video has introduced to me is Keane. Keane are a band that I was determined to dislike due to the hype and award nominations but three minutes alone with that voice was enough to change my mind completely. The combination of Tom Chaplin's pure as snow voice and those soaring choruses reminds me strongly of A-ha but there is an Englishness in their demeanour that separates them from their Norwegian counterparts. They possess an endearing humility that is quite refreshing in these me me me days and they always appear slightly bemused that anyone would want to listen to anything they did. In addition, they have opted for a slightly unorthodox line-up of piano, voice and drums that gives them a marginally old-fashioned, yet alternative sound. Many singer songwriters of the last thirty years would release ballads arranged for piano and voice and the same people would then add either a band or an orchestral setting for a more detailed sound, but no one has really used the rather stark piano and drum sound as a backdrop for all types of songs unless you count the Ben Folds Five in the mid 1990s. Unfortunately, Ben Folds tried this set up, plus bass, in the midst of the guitar dominated Brit Rock period of the Oasis and Blur wars and was so submerged. Today, Keane have surfaced in an era of slightly less aggressive sounds and following Coldplay's lead have benefited accordingly. There is no doubt that they have come up with some gorgeous tunes on their debut 'Hopes and Fears', but sadly they will need to broaden their sound if they are to avoid becoming predictable and this may blunt their individuality. I hope not.

Television technology has also allowed me to pander to my other indulgence: the Glastonbury festival, which I can enjoy unreservedly without actually having to sit in a muddy field with a telescope for three days, especially now that the BBC have expanded their coverage on their digital channels. It means that I can experience most of the major bands on the bill and still have access to a decent toilet. In the last few years I have watched hours and hours of this event as, like the folk club experience, it gives the sort of genuine insight into the capabilities of a particular artist or band that a carefully manipulated video does not. There is nothing like a live performance to rub off the glamour and falseness of the MTV presentation and there are always a few surprises. In recent years I have been unexpectedly impressed by Scissor Sisters, Ultrasound, Morcheeba and equally disappointed by others, who shall be nameless to protect the guilty. It is always refreshingly enjoyable to experience live music, whether in situ or vicariously via the television and the sheer creativity of some artists never fails to inspire me. Who can forget Alison Goldfrapp's horse's tail in 2004 or Courtney Love's carefully managed stage invasion in 1999?

However, all this technology pales into insignificance when confronted by the gizmo that is the MP3 player. I have just obtained one of these gadgets and loaded my entire CD collection onto it – a staggering concept in itself – and the idea that I can now carry this about and listen to anything I please at any time is beyond my wildest boyhood dreams. I usually set it so that it plays any track in random order, a bit like listening to your own radio station without the inane chat but often with surprising results:

'That last Coldplay album was a bit disappointing. Hmm, this intro is good.
What is it?'

(Fumbles in pocket to retrieve the machine)

'Coldplay! Damn!'

The other aspect that becomes apparent is that of relativity. When you listen to songs in a jumbled order without regard to historical period or style, certain of them stand out from their peers like rare jewels and they are not always the ones you expect. Listening to an average song from a good album amongst its colleagues often provokes no reaction at all, but hear it among unrelated songs and its quality suddenly leaps out at you. The MP3 player is causing me to re-evaluate a lot of my preconceptions about things I thought I knew.

Whilst I am still a great music store browser, the technology of the Internet has opened up the business of music purchase by a magnitude previously undreamed of. I have already spoken of my purchase of Fanny's CD box set 'The First Time in a Long Time' released through the Internet only label; Rhino Handmade and there are many artists, Sing-Sing and Aimee Mann spring to mind, who release albums through their own websites, but there are other avenues to pursue, such as the auction sites. I have made several purchases of hard to obtain albums on eBay, my last success being Judie Tzuke's 'Shoot the Moon', the CD version of which has mysteriously been deleted and is unavailable other than second-hand. I have always liked Judie Tzuke's vocal style and bought her debut 'Welcome to the Cruise' and one or two subsequent albums but 'Shoot the Moon' has always been my favourite, partly due to the song 'Liggers at Your Funeral' which voices her outrage at the false sentimentality of certain stars over Peter Sellers' death. The song is carried along by Mike Paxman's swirling guitar riff and some great jazz influenced piano. Unfortunately, my only copy of this album was a cassette purchased from a bargain bin in the late 1980s and the sound quality has been deteriorating for years. So I was very pleased to pick up a rare CD copy on eBay for £20, as previous examples had all sold in the £35–50 range reflecting its sought after status. Like buses, rare items eventually turn up again and again so if one is out of reach, it always pays to wait for the next one rather than fall into the trap of bidding over your limit.

All this is welcome news to obsessives, who buy masses of albums as part of their genetic makeup, but very few of us actually sell any. When they do, it is usually when the balance of their mind is disturbed like when yet another Status Quo album is released. I recall one acquaintance who having donated a large proportion of his record collection to the local charity shop, suddenly came to his senses and rushed back to repurchase them all. This sort of muddle-headedness has gripped me from time to time and no good came from it, I can tell you.

I have only fallen prey to the urge to sell major parts of my collection on two occasions to date, one was in about 1976 when I was student and funds were so low that drastic action was called for and the other was in the 1980s when I considered my collection too unwieldy. Quite why I should have harboured this misconception is difficult to divine now. Perhaps storage space was a problem but my overall collection is more than three times as large now, so the act appears no more than a futile gesture now. At the time, I examined all those artists where I owned more than about 2 or 3 three examples of their work and attempted to identify their best efforts with a view to selling the remainder at a second-hand shop. This meant that my Chicago collection, for example, lost Chicago 6, 7 and 8, but retained the first three albums and Chicago 5, which I considered the best. Unfortunately, Chicago 7 contains 'Wishing You Were Here', their excellent collaboration with the Beach Boys and this is now lost to me unless I re-buy the whole double album.

The merits of selling albums are easy to understand at the time of sale but more difficult to rationalise in retrospect when the reasons for sale are long forgotten. What remains is the feeling that many good albums have disappeared but this is, for the most part, false nostalgia. There are a good many albums that I have disposed of that I am happy never to have to listen to again, but inevitably there are a few others where I have relented and consequently been forced to buy for a second time. These purchases have been justified on the basis that I am replacing albums with CD copies, but this is just fooling myself. They include, amongst a disconcertingly lengthening list, The Faces' 'A Nod's as Good as a Wink' and Deep Purple's 'Burn', which were firm favourites at the time of original purchase so quite why they had to go mystifies me. The Faces' LP is the more puzzling as it had cost me a mind-numbing £2.50 at a time when LPs were generally in the £2.00–£2.25 range and Faust were on the point of releasing their infamous 'Faust Tapes' at an astoundingly low price of 49 pence. Rod Stewart obviously had his eye on a few costly divorces, even at that stage in his life.

The one saving grace that helps to sanction the act of repurchase is that I am now buying CD copies of LPs at less cost than the original purchase. An LP that cost £2.00 in 1970 should cost £22.00 today, allowing for 35 years price inflation. In fact most new CDs can be bought for £10.00 or less showing that in real terms, CDs are better value now than they ever were and many back catalogue titles can be picked up for considerably less that £10.00 making the act of repurchase somewhat less of a financial strain.

But mostly, I find that in the current age of cherry picking tracks from albums, I am buying albums again in order to own one or two favourite tracks, as in the case of Chicago 7, and this is madness but then when has record collecting ever been anything else?

But having sold and then repurchased certain albums, I have discovered that something very peculiar is at work during the period between transactions. Is it my imagination, or do albums change subtly when out of your possession? It's almost as though they take the opportunity to alter their appeal as soon as you have no control over them. Having repurchased Deep Purple's 'Burn' and brought it back into the fold, I was taken aback to find that all those tracks I loved when I first owned the album had transmuted into rather less than great songs and all those that I once hated had taken on a far more acceptable demeanour. In particular is the song, 'Mistreated', which was a rather plodding affair, as I recalled – but not any more. Now, I find it is a powerful ballad, competently sung by David Coverdale and annexed to a stunningly good guitar solo from Ritchie Blackmore. How did this happen? It's almost worth repurchasing all the albums I have sold over the years just to see what they have done with themselves whilst we have been apart.

The answer to all this heartache would be obvious to most people and that is never to sell anything at all. For the indisputable fact is that the whole of a collection, even the duff purchases, lovingly compiled over the course of a lifetime, form a diary of sorts that tracks your life, warts and all. It secures memories in the same way that a photo album reminds of events past and you wouldn't take your old photographs to the charity shop, would you?

Epilogue

It seems almost incredible that rock music has sidled past its fiftieth birthday, like an aging hell raiser now ignored by the world, without so much as a squeak when its inception was greeted by the establishment of the time with so much noisy suspicion and promises of moral corruption on a massive scale.

Ironically, during that same period there has, as predicted, been much social change but it is technology, not rock music, that has changed all our lives, irrevocably. In the sphere of music it has changed how it is created, recorded, reproduced, marketed, stored, and traded and most of it is to the good. If I had been told, aged eleven, at the time I bought my first vinyl single that in the future I would be able to carry my entire album collection around in a box no bigger than a cigarette packet, I would have laughed. But the MP3 player has made this a reality.

Perhaps the greatest change has been the use of the Internet to share knowledge and to buy and sell music. One of its most persuasive attributes is that it allows us to ignore albums and purchase single songs instantly via the medium of the music file download. As a confirmed albums buyer, this new technology with its easy accessibility, low cost and absence of filler, is slowly changing my outlook and is thus taking me back to my youth when singles were my main pursuit and albums were little more than collections of singles rather than individual art forms. It is strangely fitting that the generational changes in the technology of music have brought me full circle to the beginning of this book when seven-inch vinyl singles opened up my world and where I started out trying to pinpoint the source of my lifelong obsessions with music in the majority of its popular forms. That journey is now almost complete.

So what has been the effect of musical obsession on my life? I have patently failed to attain rock star status myself and have not even managed to know someone who has, but this is hardly surprising as few people rise to this sort of level of achievement. On the positive side, I have amassed a vast music collection and filled whole storage racks with CDs, LPs and cassettes that have given me untold pleasure. I have taught myself to play the guitar to a lowly standard and have proved to myself at least, that I can write songs of variable quality. In the scheme of things these are not bad achievements.

At the beginning of this book, I described the effects of music obsession in terms of behaviour and its consequences. Even now, I am still afflicted by the onset of all those emotions; joy, irritation, boredom, exhilaration, hope and despair, but now I am used to them and they no longer bother me like they did. I can even stand the glassy eyed stares of strangers at social events because I know, in my heart of hearts, that I am the lucky one.

In my life, music has played a major part and it still does. As John Miles puts it, a little tweely, in his song, 'Music':

'Music was my first love, and it will be my last'.

If anything, I can be more deeply moved now than at any time in the past and I consider this to be a great gift. It is, perhaps, no surprise that these days I no longer become enthused by every other song that comes my way as it did thirty odd years ago, but there are still occasional instances where that familiar adrenaline rush accompanies the discovery of something new. The Killers' 'Somebody Told Me' is one such recent discovery that leaves me breathless just as the Beatles did back in 1963 and countless others since and I fervently hope that the experience never ceases.

I am glad to report that there are instances where the thought of music almost takes me over and if I am away from home, say at work or visiting, I will have an urge to return home and play the song or album that has been calling to me so insistently. There have been long periods where I have listened to music every day without fail. Certainly there have been times when, just like the cliché, music has been the soundtrack to my life and it has comforted in times of despair and exhilarated in times of joy. On the plus side, being bitten by the bug has given me some of my best experiences, be it listening to albums or live gigs or watching televised performances. The negative side can usually be summed up by my failure to enthuse others about the merits of a new band or worse, requiring attendance at a live performance which failed to enthral and being left with that feeling that you have made a fool of yourself, but overall it has not been a bad experience.

Accordingly, it occurs to me that, rather than banish the bug, I ought to pass it on. If there is anything I would like to bequeath to my children it is that I would love to instil in them a love of music. I really don't mind whether it entails learning to play a musical instrument or being able to sing or just to appreciate music for its own sake, but I would like music to mean something to them as it has to me. If, in addition, I can impart to them an appreciation of its history and the people who made it, that would be a bonus but if not, no matter.

The difficulty in enthusing new generations of potential music lovers is not just that there are a multitude of other things to occupy them, but that rock music is now so old. It is those fifty years since Bill Haley and Elvis Presley sounded the warning shots in the battle for our acceptance of the new form that will create an increasingly insurmountable barrier. There is a history to be learned and that requires effort. It was easy for me as rock 'n' roll was my life almost from the day I was born. I lived through its development and assimilated it without thinking but today, rock becomes a subject to be learned like history or English literature and that takes not only interest, but also academic commitment. Think of the hundreds of classic albums that need to be experienced before a real understanding of our heritage is formulated. For today's generations, that means time and money. It's a lot to ask and recalling my own reluctance to delve into the mysteries of hundreds of years of classical music, I'm not sure I would want to do it, so why should they?

The evidence of this loss of connection is all around, but never more so than in the various television music quiz shows where musicians and commentators alike, parade their lack of knowledge under cover of alternative comedy. It saddens me that people who form bands today do so without any appreciation of the heritage of their chosen profession, and only seem to look towards the rewards it may bring. Of course, there will always be those who choose musicianship from a love of music and it is difficult to know whether to applaud or pity them for, in today's materialistic society, where the majority are looking more towards their own 15 minutes of fame at the expense of the rest, they are likely to flounder.

There was a telling moment that occurred during the Brit Awards recently. In the course of a television discussion amongst 'music experts', each was asked to say a few words about the nominations for best album, which included Brian Wilson's long awaited release of the Beach Boys' 'Smile' (an album that had been shelved in 1967 but had been finally completed by Brian after some 37 years!) and a release from Tom Waites. One 'expert' admitted that he didn't actually know who Brian Wilson or Tom Waites was and was thus unable to comment. With so little knowledge of our pop heritage, what was this person doing on the programme? Sometimes the mud with 'dumbing down' etched into it, does occasionally stick and the pandering to inexperienced youth over quality is laid bare.

But there is hope. Amongst the few, one who has impressed me enormously is Lauren Laverne, one time member of the 1990s band Kenickie and now a broadcaster, who seems to have a real enthusiasm and a depth of understanding of music past and present and this is refreshingly commendable in one so young. A second note of encouragement is borne by the vast crowds that pack the summer festivals to see both new and old bands alike and show no distaste at singing along with songs that, for the most part, their parents knew in their youth. Perhaps not all is lost.

But, given all the difficulties involved, it now seems more important than ever that our musical heritage is not forgotten. Accordingly, I would still wish to impart some level of appreciation and if I can achieve a flicker of interest in my own children without alienating them, I feel I will have fulfilled my duty on earth.

But then, kids never do what you want, do they?

Appendix

TWENTY-FIVE ALBUMS (Plus one)

For no other reason than I like lists, here are twenty-five (well, twenty-six actually because there's always more than you can handle and I couldn't bear to leave one out) of my favourite albums, chosen on the basis that I own them and play them a lot.

1.   The Zombies – Odessey and Oracle (1968)

Unlike the Americans, the British public had long given up on the Zombies but Rod Argent and Chris White's unheralded masterpiece is a Pandora's box of psychedelic melodies and masterful arrangements. Its diversity runs the gamut from the uplifting 'Time of the Season' to the chilling 'Butcher's Tale (Western Front 1914)'. The fact that Colin Blunstone went to the same school as me, albeit some ten years apart, has no bearing on this selection.

2.   Chicago – Chicago II (1970)

Chicago's prodigious early output sprawled across their first three double albums with unfettered abandon. This, their second, contains the usual mix of styles from chunks of infectiously energetic jazz rock and orchestral chamber pieces to protest rock and pop songs. All topped off with Terry Kath's irrepressible guitar. This is how they should be remembered.

3.   Fanny – Fanny (1970)

Fanny's pioneering story of girl power in a man's world starts here with a compelling argument that women could play rock 'n' roll as well as anybody else. The playing is superb and the writing inventive. The Canadian version, pressed from the wrong master tapes and containing earlier work, is even better. Even David Bowie is a fan. Funky but feminine.

4. Jethro Tull – Aqualung (1971)

Ian Anderson's folk inclinations show through in the acoustic 'Wond'ring Aloud' and 'Slipstream' but the whole album is really a collection of folk songs, giving voice to Anderson's opinionated rantings in the minstrel tradition and transposed into a rock setting by some typically complex rhythm work and Martin Barre's buzzing guitar.

5. Curved Air – Second Album (1971)

Progressive rock at its best and hardly a guitar in sight. Haunting melodies are juxtaposed with electronic and string settings to give a unique platform for Sonja Kristina's serene vocals. The epic 12-minute 'Piece of Mind' is arguably the best thing they ever did. Sonja's spoken lines from T.S. Eliot's poem, 'The Waste Land' over a piano and violin theme still raises the hairs on my neck even now.

6. Focus – Focus 3 (1972)

A double album of Bach fugues, extended bluesy guitar jams and yodelling, all in a single package. The only LP I own that has a single track that plays for a whole side and then continues on the next. Genuine musicianship without a style consultant in sight and all the better for it. The mutated beast that is Euro rock.

7. Joni Mitchell – For the Roses (1972)

Perhaps the finest lyricist of her generation and not a bad tunesmith either. Vivid sound portraits of everyday happenings made real by the incisive truths revealed. A work of real depth and beauty plus the bonus of quality piano playing. None of your two finger doodling here.

8.   Yes – Tales from Topographic Oceans (1973)

Although universally derided, this is my favourite Yes album. Despite the absence of killer three-minute songs, it is inventively constructed and contains some thrilling themes. Who else do you know that has the capacity to conceive, write and arrange four twenty-minute pieces of popular music, even if the lyrics are complete gibberish?

9.   Steeleye Span – Parcel of Rogues (1973)

Maddy and the classic Span line-up at the peak of their powers before the addition of a standard rock drummer and 'All Around My Hat'. A careful selection of centuries old folk songs skilfully arranged for both traditional and rock instruments plus one of the finest voices in English folk. Such a shame that the call of commerciality overcame them.

10. Split Enz – Mental Notes (1976)

Bonkers rock from down under. An object lesson in how good songs can be made better by truly original musical arrangements and not worrying too much about the result. Based in folk music, this is as diverse an album as you will ever hear. Better than Crowded House.

11. Talking Heads – More Songs about Buildings and Food (1978)

Archetypal stuttering, quirky vocals from David Byrne over the pin-sharp rhythms of husband and wife drum 'n' bass team Chris Frantz and Tina Weymouth. A majestic cover of Al Green's 'Take Me to the River' reveals that the band is not just a one-trick pony. A consummate marriage between the energy of the new wave and true eccentricity.

12. Jane Aire and the Belvederes (1979)

I know virtually nothing about Jane Aire other than I like this ragbag of ballads, updated Motown songs and unusual rockers. Her deep vibrant voice is ideally suited to the character of the album and her backing band (including drummer Jon Moss, later of Culture Club) is exemplary.

13. The Cure – Seventeen Seconds (1980)

In the wake of punk came the Cure and an album that is nothing to do with manic guitars and sneering vocals but all about glacial songs and sparse atmospheric backdrops. Robert Smith's lost little boy vocals are awash with paranoia and his echoing guitar spawned a hundred imitators.

14. The Passions – 30,000 Feet Over China (1981)

Probably how a marginally more cheerful Cure would sound with a female vocalist. Barbara Gogan's vocal similarity to Robert Smith is coincidental but the standard guitar, bass and drums configuration never sounded so good. The variety of the song writing manages to keep the interest up in the face of rather samey arrangements.

15. Judie Tzuke – Shoot the Moon (1982)

Having left Elton John's Rocket label, Judie's first album for Chrysalis is a cracker. Her exuberant soprano provides a shimmering façade to a bunch of quality songs as she looks towards a career rejuvenation. Shame that more label hopping eventually drained the promise of this album. Her best effort since her debut 'Welcome to the Cruise' which was also a contender for this list.

16. Kate Bush – The Dreaming (1982)

A real star is born. Kate comes of age with this self-produced, delicate yet sometimes impenetrable offering. The precursor to 'Hounds of Love', it is boundlessly imaginative, although sometimes the execution struggles to keep pace. Overall a fascinating album showing the promise to come.

17. The Smiths – Hatful of Hollow (1984)

The partnership of Johnny Marr's complex guitar parts and Morrissey's wry yet poignant lyrics were never bettered than on this collection of sessions for John Peel's radio show. The raw live feel seems to suit the band as they outperform the studio versions of the same songs with a vengeance.

18. Propaganda – A Secret Wish (1985)

Trevor Horn's mega 80s production may sound a little overblown now but the relentless rhythms and sheer oddity of this band make it a unique snapshot of a place in history. 'Duel' still boasts the unsettling combination of a life-affirming tune and unspeakably violent lyrics.

19. A-ha – Scoundrel Days (1986)

The teeny bop stars grow up with this collection of stirring ballads and electronic rock. Unlike their electronic genre peers, they used a live drummer rather than the newly invented drum machine and this propels the storming 'I've Been Losing You' into my list of all time favourite songs. Outdoor listening essential.

20. All About Eve – Scarlet and Other Stories (1989)

Grandiose arrangements and Julianne Regan's cut-glass vocals make this album one to listen to with a glass of vintage champagne. A sort of goth/prog mix that draws from both folk and heavy metal and overlays the mix with gorgeous melodies. 'Only One Reason' is one of the most haunting songs I know.

21. Madonna – Like a Prayer (1989)

Madonna's real talent is not singing, but a knack of surrounding herself with the right people at the right time. Here, Pat Leonard, fresh from his success as collaborator on the preceding album 'True Blue', co-writes some of her best work, which includes the emotionally charged, gospel tinged title track and the autobiographical 'Oh Father'. A rite of passage album.

22. Julian Cope – Jehovahkill (1992)

Despite Cope's outwardly eccentric image, he still understands that at the root of all great pop music is a good tune and this album contains loads of them. Better still, they are attached to weird lyrical stories and self-depreciating humour. An album to savour whilst sitting in your own stone circle.

23. Juliana Hatfield – Become What You Are (1993)

Juliana packed in her bass guitar job with Evan Dando's Lemonheads, got herself a noisy guitar and made a series of loose, tuneful albums on her own account. This is the best of them containing fearless rockers and reflective ballads all delivered in her little girl voice. If you like Sheryl Crow, you'll prefer this.

24. Lush – Split (1994)

The album that should have sent Lush into the premier league but their singles were always a bit of an acquired taste so they lost out on goal difference. Great pop songs set into aural soundscapes that only a shoegazing band could envisage. A great loss to the music world but their legacy lives on in this spirited album.

25. REM – Reveal (2001)

This is as near to a modern version of the Beach Boys' 'Pet Sounds' as you are likely to hear. Beautiful melodies and symphonic arrangements abound in this slightly wistful album. There is a consistency of quality here that, although not quite their best, makes this a pleasure to listen to all the way through. How many albums can you say that about these days?

26. Keane – Hopes and Fears (2004)

It is always difficult to include albums that have only just appeared, as there has been no time to appraise them with any degree of perspective, but this collection of fresh, highly melodic songs deserves the benefit of the doubt. Underpinned by some poignant piano and stirring drums, Tom Chaplin's soulful voice soars and dips in heartrending style.

Index